T0374295

Legal Risk Management
for In-House Counsel
and Managers

A MANAGER'S GUIDE TO LEGAL AND
CORPORATE RISK MANAGEMENT

Bryan E. Hopkins

PARTRIDGE

A Penguin Random House Company

Copyright © 2014 by Bryan E. Hopkins.

Library of Congress Control Number:		2014937439
ISBN:	Hardcover	978-1-4828-9637-4
	Softcover	978-1-4828-9636-7
	eBook	978-1-4828-9638-1

All rights reserved. No part of this book may be used or reproduced by any means, graphic, electronic, or mechanical, including photocopying, recording, taping or by any information storage retrieval system without the written permission of the publisher except in the case of brief quotations embodied in critical articles and reviews.

Because of the dynamic nature of the Internet, any web addresses or links contained in this book may have changed since publication and may no longer be valid. The views expressed in this work are solely those of the author and do not necessarily reflect the views of the publisher, and the publisher hereby disclaims any responsibility for them.

Print information available on the last page.

To order additional copies of this book, contact
Toll Free 800 101 2657 (Singapore)
Toll Free 1 800 81 7340 (Malaysia)
orders.singapore@partridgepublishing.com

www.partridgepublishing.com/singapore

To my wonderful wife Yeong Hee, my son Geoffrey, and daughter Christine who are always in my thoughts-thank you for your love

To Rod Manning, Esq., a fabulous lawyer and good friend

To Won Young, Won Kyung, Justin, Andrew, and others I have mentored or helped along the way— keep up the good work and pass it on

TABLE OF CONTENTS

Preface   xiii

Part 1: About Legal Risk Management   1
  1. What Is Legal Risk Management (LRM)?   3
  2. Applying Legal Risk Management in a Corporate
      Setting   5
  3. Legal Risk Management and Corporate Governance   7
      3.1 US Obligations   7
      3.2 Fiduciary Oversight   8
  4. Legal Risk Management   9
  5. Legal Risk Management and Litigation   11
  Summary   15

Part 2: Implementation of Legal Risk Management   17
  6. Legal Risk Assessment and Evaluation   19
      6.1 Risk Assessment   19
      6.2 Risk Assessment Evaluation   21
  7. Conducting Legal Risk Assessment   23
      7.1 Phases   24
  8. General Product Liability Considerations and
      Risk Management   27
      8.1 Product Liability Concerns and Costs   27
      8.2 Sources of Product Liability Risk   30
      8.3 Possible Defenses to Product Liability Exposure 31

8.4	Loss Control	33
9.	**New Product Planning and Development Management**	**37**
9.1	Stages	37
9.3	Standardization	40
9.4	Development Implementation (Including Design Verification and Production Validation)	41
9.5	Production Readiness	41
9.6	Mitigating Legal Risk in New Product Development and Planning	42
10.	**Design Risk Management**	**45**
10.1	Product Design Issues and Considerations	45
10.2	Labeling	47
10.3	Marketing Literature and Review of Manuals	50
10.4	Manufacturing and Distribution Issues	54
11.	**Risk Insurance**	**59**
11.1	Insurance Considerations: Risk Assessment	59
11.2	Coverage	60
11.3	Costs	61
11.4	Insurance Analysis	62
11.5	Evaluation of Insurance Providers	62
11.6	Creating a Captive Insurance Company	63
11.7	What Are the Primary Reasons to Consider a Captive Insurance Company?	64
12.	**Credit Risk Management**	**67**
12.1	Credit Risk	67
12.2	Credit Risk Processes	68
12.3	Credit Risk Insurance	69
12.4	Put Agreements	72
12.5	Factoring	72
13.	**Data Privacy and Risk Management**	**73**
13.1	Personal Data	74
13.2	Data Processing	75
13.3	Other Data	75
13.4	Data Processes and Related Risks	76
13.5	LRM Solutions to the Data Problem	77

14. Contract Management		**79**
14.1	Contract Risk Management	79
14.2	Contract Management Processes	82
14.3	Miscellaneous Issues	86
15. Foss		**89**
15.1	What Is FOSS?	89
15.2	Licenses	90
15.3	FOSS Violations	90
15.4	FOSS Compliance	91
16. Outsourcing		**93**
16.1	Structure	94
16.2	Outsourcing Arrangements	94
16.3	Issues and Concerns	95
16.4	Dispute Resolution	97
Summary		99

Part 3: Legal Risk Management Strategies: Pre-litigation		**101**
17. Employee Benefit Plans		**103**
17.1	Employee Benefit Plans Audit	103
17.2	Employee Benefit Plans Review	104
17.3	Fiduciary Considerations	104
17.4	Settlor Considerations	106
17.5	Plan Documents, Process, Procedures and Reporting	106
17.6	Compliance Audit	107
17.7	Recommended Actions	108
17.8	Compliance Considerations	108
18. Compliance		**109**
18.1	What Is Compliance?	109
18.2	Establishment of Compliance Program	112
18.3	Training Programs	116
18.4	Risk Assessment of Compliance Programs	117
18.5	Legal Risk Management Reasons for a Compliance Program	117
19. Record Retention		**121**
19.1	Information Retention	121

19.2 Risk Assessment: A Suggested Action 123
19.3 E-mail 123
19.4 Action Plan 124
20. Management of E-mail **127**
20.1 Management 128
20.2 Training 129
20.3 E-mail Issues 130
21. E-discovery **131**
21.1 What Is E-discovery? 131
21.2 E-discovery Obligations: US Laws and
Case Law 132
21.3 Information Technology (IT) 134
21.4 Management of E-discovery Process 135
22. Document Management **139**
22.1 The Corporate Landscape 139
22.2 Electronic Evidence 140
22.3 ESI Requirements 142
22.4 Plan of Action 143
22.5 ESI Implementation 144
23. Identification of Legal Risk **145**
23.1 Kinds of Legal Risk 145
23.2 How to Identify Legal Risk 147
24. Implementation of a Crisis Management Strategy **151**
24.1 Crisis Defined 151
24.2 Crisis Management Strategy 153
24.3 International Crisis 155
24.4 Communication Components of a Crisis
Management Plan 156
24.5 Considerations 156
25. Crisis Management: Hypothetical Case in Point **159**
Summary 163

Part 4: Legal Risk Management and Litigation **165**
26. Corporate Structure Issues **167**
26.1 Holding Company: Liability Containment 167

26.2 Centralized Management of Regulatory
  Matters Applicable to Subsidiaries and the
  Group or Parent as a Whole   168
26.3 Potential Issues Involving Holding Companies   170
27. Use of Outside Counsel   **173**
27.1 Centralization   174
**28. Picking the Law Firm: The Value Added
Proposition**   **177**
28.1 Finding Law Firms   178
28.2 Thoughts on Selecting the Appropriate
  Law Firm   179
29. US litigation   **183**
29.1 Discovery   183
29.2 Jury Trials   184
29.3 Absence of Fee-Shifting Statutes   185
29.4 Strategy   185
29.5 Class Actions   186
29.6 LRM: US Litigation   186
30. Legal Fees and Costs   **189**
30.1 Tools for Reducing Legal Fees   189
31. Litigation: Hypothetical Case in Point   **191**
32. Management of Outside Counsel   **195**
32.1 Cost Containment Strategies   195
32.2 Outside Billing Guidelines   196
32.3 Monthly Reporting   197
33. Use of Negotiations   **199**
33.1 What Are Negotiations?   199
33.2 Stages of Negotiations   199
33.3 Miscellaneous Issues   204
34. Negotiation: Hypothetical Case in Point   **205**
35. Use of Arbitration and Dispute Resolution   **209**
35.1 What Is Arbitration?   209
35.2 Justification for Arbitration   210
35.3 Arbitration Process: General Characteristics   212
35.4 Arbitral Institutions   214
35.5 Arbitration Clause   215

36. Arbitration: Hypothetical Case in Point   217
37. Management of Litigation   221
   37.1 Kinds of Actions   222
   37.2 Litigation Management Tools   223
38. Litigation Management during Trial   225
   38.1 Evaluation of the Case   226
   38.2 Fees during Litigation   227
   38.3 Evaluation of Discovery Costs during Trial   227
   38.4 To Settle or Not Settle?   228
   38.5 Evaluation of the Trial   228
   Summary   231

Part 5: Legal Risk Management: Evaluation of the Process   233
39. Legal Risk Management: Evaluation of the Process   235
   39.1 Selling Legal Risk Management to the
      Organization   235
   39.2 Quantify the Legal Exposure   236
   39.3 A "Teaching Moment"   236
40. Internalization of Legal Risk Management   239
41. Review of Legal Risk Management: Justification   241
   Summary   243

Conclusion   245
About the Author   247
Appendix A   249
Appendix B   261
Bibliography   277

PREFACE

Risk management has become popular in recent years due to various corporate scandals, government investigations, disasters, and fines. Though some in the risk management industry often refer to enterprise risk management (ERM) when discussing risk management, it is my opinion that risk management is in reality a process to reduce and minimize the legal risk that is found in many areas. Such legal issues include class actions, product liability claims and lawsuits, government investigations and fines, shareholder actions, and often other legal-related matters. Hence, this book is really about the study of legal and corporate risk or legal risk management (LRM) and what issues, concerns, processes, and procedures should be discussed and implemented when instituting a legal risk management program.

The main role of in-house counsel in corporations or legal entities is, of course, to mitigate legal risk in connection with the sale of products or services provided by the company. In essence how the company protects its success will be based in part on its ability to manage, control, and minimize legal risk, especially in a litigious society such as the US marketplace. Legal counsel must take an active effort in developing strategies, systems, and processes that will minimize the legal risks faced by the company on a daily basis.

In order for the LRM program to be successful in any organization, management must be involved. It is hoped that corporate managers will also take an interest in this vital area, as a successful risk management program or LRM program greatly depends on executive ownership of risk management. Only with the buy-in of executive management will legal risk management be embedded in the strategic decision-making processes of the organization.

It is hoped, therefore, that this book will not only aid in-house counsel when dealing with legal risk management issues but will also help educate managers and corporate managers as to the issues and concerns of legal risk they face, but also potential strategies, processes, and procedures when dealing with legal risk management or LRM.

This book describes many of the processes and activities that have been developed through my experience to manage and control legal risks faced by most companies today. It is not meant to be exhaustive or all-encompassing, but to describe the basic LRM processes a risk manager, corporate manager, or in-house counsel should consider when trying to minimize legal risk and exposure.

It should be noted that I will often refer to legal risk management as the acronym LRM throughout this book. I cannot emphasize enough the fact that risk management itself is interconnected with legal risk. All risk management issues at the end are connected to and quantifiable by the legal exposure faced by a company. Therefore, for a company to protect its bottom line, an aggressive LRM program should be implemented on a daily basis.

This book is intended as an introduction to legal risk management to be used by corporate counsel, risk managers, or managers in general and should be used for educational purposes. I refer to risk management principles, insurance concepts, and basic corporate concepts throughout the book as issues that intersect and connect with legal risk management.

The concepts in this book reflect my experience in managing the numerous legal risks for multinationals. This book is not intended to be an exhaustive legal treatise or a legal hornbook but merely a guide to be used by those in-house or corporate managers. I leave a detailed legal analysis one would expect in a treatise or hornbook to others. Because this is an introduction to legal risk management and not an exhaustive textbook or treatise, I will not refer to the multitude of books and articles written on the various topics of this book but will limit the references I use. Nonetheless, I obviously owe a great deal to the practitioners and authors who have influenced me. However, I must state that the greatest teacher I have had over the years has actually been experience. It is my experience that I offer to you, the reader. Needless to say, I hope this book becomes the basis for further discussion and analysis on the topics presented.

At the beginning of many chapters in this book I list proposed forms, checklists, and other tools that should be considered in implementing a LRM program. A few will be set forth in the appendixes of this book. However, as the forms I list are quite numerous, most cannot be included in this book but will have to wait for another book and another day.

This book is divided into five parts, with part 1 introducing LRM and the other parts discussing the LRM process. I have added several hypothetical case studies at the end of major chapters to help put legal risk in context and help the reader appreciate the seriousness and complexity of LRM processes and procedures that one faces in an attempt to mitigate and control legal risk. Remember, the fate of a company or organization in today's world is tied to how it handles legal risk and whether it manages risk effectively or fails to appreciate the consequences of disregarding it.

It is in this spirit that I humbly offer this book.

B. E. Hopkins

PART 1

About Legal Risk Management

1

What Is Legal Risk Management (LRM)?

The focus of legal risk management or LRM is to control and manage an organization's legal risks, which in countries such as the United States are numerous and diverse. Legal risk management processes are primarily designed and implemented to engage in preventative projects, such as counseling the organization regarding insurance matters, developing risk management processes, and administering training programs, as well as involvement with legal defense activities, such as coordinating the company's defenses against product safety litigation and claims, responding to product-related investigations, and analyzing governmental reporting responsibilities vis-à-vis the company's various products. In fact, a compliance program can be considered part of the LRM process, as it can be an effective tool to monitor and prevent actions that are either against corporate policies or that are illegal. As you can see, it is a broad and important function that encompasses many areas.

By controlling and managing legal risk, an organization is able to control its future. Without adequate LRM processes, a company is exposed to claims, lawsuits, fines, and investigations. Not a day goes by where some governmental investigation or lawsuit is not reported in the local newspaper. These days it is a common occurrence. Therefore, it is imperative that an organization understands the role that LRM plays in an organization and that adequate systems, processes, and procedures be implemented to minimize, control, and transfer such legal risk.

2

Applying Legal Risk Management
in a Corporate Setting

Legal risk management processes and procedures must be applied to provide risk management expertise and to prevent loss due to claims, litigation, and investigations and fines. LRM, when properly applied in a corporate setting, whether under the control of the company's law department or under the control of a separate division such as compliance or insurance, should cover general areas of responsibility or functions such as:

- Periodic risk assessment of the company's operating divisions and departments, and reporting the results to management
- Developing solutions to risk management issues
- Advising the corporation on insurance coverage issues and potential alternatives for coverage
- Oversight of the company's defense of product safety litigation and claims and advise management and legal on a regular basis on product safety matters
- Monitoring of product safety issues and analyzing the need for governmental reporting and/or taking corrective action

- Oversight of the company's information and document retention program
- Compliance review
- Development of training programs
- Monitoring compliance issues
- Training the company's employees on risk management, product safety, and often various legal issues such as antitrust, product liability or intellectual property (IP) issues

In order to apply LRM in a company or corporate setting, legal and management must take an active role in applying the above areas of responsibility through processes or systems implemented within the company. Normally, a Risk Management Department (RMD) will be established separately or in Legal, Compliance, or other divisions that will have certain risk management functions, responsibilities, or mandates across the company or organization as a whole.

The issues facing many companies when dealing with legal risk management, whether through a stand-alone department—RMD—or within Legal or Compliance, is that divisions and/or departments within a corporation often fail to effectively partner with RMD. This, in turn, leads to improper handling of major legal and sensitive issues, which can lead to legal claims, fines, and liabilities. Legal missteps can lead to a major crisis. Therefore, the LRM process must be properly implemented in a corporation. Such implementation is discussed in a more detailed fashion in part 2 of this book.

3

Legal Risk Management and Corporate Governance

3.1 US Obligations

Risk management as part of good corporate governance has become popular in many countries due to recent scandals such as Worldcom and Enron. Due to such scandals, the Sarbanes-Oxley Act (SOX) was introduced in the United States in 2002. SOX requires, among other things, that proper internal financial controls be established in publicly traded companies as well as whistleblower provisions and compliance policies. In fact the U.S. laws and regulations regarding compliance requires that the board of directors are not only trained in compliance but also has compliance oversight. Similar measures have been passed in other jurisdictions as well.

The result of SOX and other laws in other jurisdictions was to force upon the board of directors the obligation of ensuring the proper financial controls are in place and that such controls would be properly followed and maintained.[1]

---

[1] Paul M. Collier, *Fundamentals of Risk Management for Accountants and Managers*, (Elsevier, 2009), 15–19.

As such, risk management processes in general should be considered by the board of directors in light of the board's fiduciary and legal responsibilities.

3.2 Fiduciary Oversight

Legal risk management not only plays an important part in the success or failure of a corporation, but it is so important that it must be elevated to the board of directors for such LRM processes to be effective. As the board of directors of a company owes a fiduciary duty and obligation to the corporation, such duty requires a board of directors (BOD) that is fully informed and knowledgeable on major issues of risk. Whether it is ERISA issues, compliance issues, SOX, currency risk, antitrust, M&A issues, etc., the BOD must be fully informed to make the appropriate decisions involving the management of the company. Due to its very nature, the BOD cannot escape its fiduciary obligations with regard to understanding and approving LRM processes.

Obviously, to protect the board as well as officers from frivolous lawsuits, including shareholder actions, a company should purchase directors and officers insurance (D&O insurance). Whether to purchase D&O insurance is a question that must be decided in the context of legal risk management. Good corporate governance requires the board to be fully informed as to the major risk issues facing the company. D&O insurance may be necessary to protect the BOD as well as executive management from lawsuits stemming from fiduciary responsibilities or lack thereof.

Failure to properly elevate risk issues to the board level is not only a failure of proper corporate governance but of LRM processes as well. Authority to implement many LRM processes must come from the BOD of a company, or its counterpart in other organizational forms. Therefore, failure to properly inform the BOD on LRM related issues can spell disaster.

4

Legal Risk Management

Minimizing legal risk or the exposure of legal risk takes place in several stages, basically, several stages prior to potential litigation or pre-litigation and, of course, during litigation as well. Obviously, minimizing legal risk even during pre-litigation is a proactive or preventative stage in which risk management processes are implemented in order to reduce the risk of lawsuits or government investigations, fines, or penalties.

This stage of LRM can be considered in essence a stage where the company can take an "proactive" approach to legal concerns and prevent potential exposure. This stage can cover areas such as:

- Prelaunch product review: What processes are in place to look at a product's historical data prior to its launch in the marketplace?
- Product safety: If a company produces products, what processes are in place to minimize claims, recalls, class action, CPSC settlements, and fines?
- Product risk management: What processes are in place to encourage correct product use, increase customer satisfaction, and manage possible injury from its use? This also includes improving the ability of the company to

defend itself by substantiating defenses to liability, reducing exposure to liability, and assisting in regular compliance.

- Insurance: What processes are in place to review the company's insurance coverage? This includes assessments of availability/policy limits, relationships with insurance cost benefit analysis of premiums, and alternatives for coverage such as creating a captive insurance company.
- Information/document retention program: A major issue for companies dealing with the United States in any capacity is the creation and use of a document retention program. What processes are in place to implement a robust document retention policy, which minimizes fines, penalties, or sanctions during litigation? The program must be in place before litigation to adequately protect the company.
- Risk management assessments of critical departments within the corporation: What processes, if any, have been developed to assess the risk factors of major departments or divisions, such as Human Resources?
- Compliance: A properly implemented compliance program can have a great impact on corporate liability and exposure to legal risk. What processes, if any, have been put in place to develop a compliance program? Does one exist?

5

Legal Risk Management and Litigation

Legal risk management plays a vital role during litigation as well. LRM processes should drive a company's defense during litigation, especially litigation in the United States. Such processes should play a major role in coordinating a company's defenses against product safety litigation and claims, responding to government investigations, and product-related or service-related investigations.

It should be noted that processes developed to defend against litigation must take into consideration a number of issues, especially if more than one division or subsidiary is subject to potential litigation in the United States or elsewhere. Such processes should include the following litigation considerations, especially these companies or divisions operating in the U.S. marketplace.

- Multiple group companies can be named as defendants. These companies will need coordination of defense and discovery matters.
- Maintaining corporate compliance.
- Litigation respecting same products in multiple jurisdictions.
- Insurance coverage: Is it adequate? Risk Management or Legal needs to review insurance coverage.

- Communication: Are communication protocols set up to facilitate effective and efficient communication between relevant departments, especially in case of a crisis?
- Internal Investigations: Is there a complaint and investigation procedure protocol?
- Centralized management of litigation must be implemented for:
    - Effective coordination of legal defense efforts in order for the companies and attorneys to avoid duplication of cost and effort from case to case.
    - Coordinated use of witnesses, answers and interrogatory responses, documents, deposition materials, and research and briefs on legal issues.
    - Assurance of consistency of actions taken at every phase of the litigation, including pleadings, discovery and responses, discovery motions, and settlement strategies.
    - Proper minimization of disruptions to the company's business by internally coordinating fact-finding.
    - Development, implementation, and coordination of a defense plan.
    - Coordinated activity regarding PR.
    - Coordinated activity respecting financial considerations, such as:
        - Reserves
        - Disclosure to auditors

For cases where multiple group companies are named as defendants or where actions respecting the same product are filed in multiple jurisdictions, an effective litigation management process can provide a central site for:

- Preservation of evidence, documents, files, and records
- Use of document depositories and computerized storage
- Coordinated or cross-referenced numbering system for documents

- Coordination of protective orders and procedures for handling claims of confidentiality and privilege

An LRM program must also:

- Establish complaints and claims handling procedures and controls.
- Establish claims processing procedures.
- Establish record-keeping guidelines.
- Establish e-discovery process controls.

From the above, it is apparent that the role legal risk management should play in litigation is important. Only a well-thought-out LRM program that considers all the above-mentioned issues and concerns will be successful.

SUMMARY

LRM focuses on processes that control, manage, and mitigate an organization's legal exposure. The processes can be preventive in nature, such as training or implementation of insurance programs. An example of a preventive process would be the implementation of a compliance program. This can minimize fines, lawsuits, and investigations.

To be successful, LRM processes need to be properly applied in an organization's structure. If applied in a corporate setting, such processes should be controlled by the Law Department or Risk Management Department covering such areas as oversight of product safety issues, insurance coverage, and compliance. The RMD or Law Department must take an active role managing risk management functions and applying such programs.

The mandate to apply and manage LRM processes usually comes from executive management, including the board of directors. To be effective, the BOD must authorize and approve such programs. Hence, the BOD can only do so when fully informed on the necessity of such programs.

LRM processes take place in stages, normally prior to litigation (pre-litigation) or during lawsuits or investigations (the litigation stage) and claims. During pre-litigation, the company can take an "offensive" approach to prevent claims, such as the use of insurance or product risk management programs. Otherwise, LRM processes can be used during litigation in a more reactive manner, such as using tools to centralize and manage litigation in order to control costs.

PART 2

Implementation of Legal Risk Management

6

Legal Risk Assessment and Evaluation

6.1 Risk Assessment

In order to implement a legal risk management (LRM) program that mitigates legal risk, manages product claims, and ensures the timely escalation and handling of risk-related issues, it is imperative to conduct a risk assessment and evaluation of the findings of such risk assessment. Many companies have in fact some risk management processes in place, but usually only a few, and those processes are not well coordinated. The basic implementation of risk management takes place in phases as follows:

RISK MANAGEMENT SOPHISTICATION

Phase 1	Some sporadic risk management activities
Phase 2	Routine risk management activities
Phase 3	Enterprise-wide risk monitoring activities
Phase 4	Risk management becomes part of the overall strategic process

It is only through adoption of a comprehensive risk management program and routine that a company can begin to not only identify major areas of legal risk but implement a fully integrated risk management structure that coordinates all enterprise risk management (ER) activities.

Risk assessments would include a review of all critical corporate processes and procedures, with an evaluation of the weaknesses of the current processes. The risk assessments would cover such areas as:

- All insurance matters, including the renewal of insurance carrier and recommending obtaining additional or different types of insurance when needed.
- Handling all product liability claims, including product safety claims, subrogation claims, investigations, discovery, and product liability lawsuits for the organization.
- Reviewing product warranties, warnings, and manuals to ensure compliance with US laws and regulations.
- Reviewing processes regarding product recalls, government-related complaints, and government investigations and inquiries, including CPSC and FTC in the United States, etc.
- Working with the Service Department or QA Department and other departments to analysis potential safety issues and report the findings to the loss-control committee in order to prevent problems before they can expand.
- Performing due diligence reviews of safety-related issues and evaluating such findings.
- Reviewing PR/marketing processes, other departments and outside PR on responding to the media with respect to safety-related issues (media crisis team/crisis management team).
- Assessing the training given to the service/call center (if any) personnel on how to handle consumers complaining about safety issues and how to recognize product liability issues and escalate them to the proper people.

- Review and assess processes and procedures of any testing labs of facilities the company may have. Governmental agencies, such as the CPSC in the United States, do not give companies much time to respond to inquiries and expect testing facilities to conduct tests in a timely and efficient manner.

6.2 Risk Assessment Evaluation

In evaluating risk assessments in order to minimize legal risk, specific goals or objectives should be established in which to evaluate or judge the risk assessments that have been completed. Such goals or objectives for a consumer product manufacturing company could be as set forth in the hypothetical scenario below:

6.2.1 Objectives

The proposed LRM plan of the XXX Company set forth herein intends to accomplish the following objectives:
- Contain and minimize the company's per-matter legal expenses and exposure.
- Streamline and strengthen the function of the company's Service Department and enhance its value.
- Implement a strong auditing program to review and analyze product complaints and failures, and evaluate corrective action and governmental reporting.
- Develop a cooperative working relationship with the Consumer Products Safety Commission (CPSC), for purposes of better dealing with future CPSC investigations and actions involving the company or its divisions.
- Contain and minimize product recalls.
- Conduct a global review of the company's insurance-related situation, including assessments of availability/policy limits, relationships with the insurers, cost-benefit analyses of premiums, and alternatives for coverage.

- Implement a process for conducting substantive legal reviews of product warnings and warranties to standardize, improve, and minimize exposure arising from product literature.
- Work with other related companies or subsidiaries, including other divisions or sister companies, to coordinate the defense of safety/product liability claims against the parent company.
- Implement and aggressively monitor company's document retention policy.

6.2.2 Processes

- Revise procedures for identifying and processing claims (in-house and through the company's insurer) that foster efficiency and retention by Legal of greater oversight and control over claims processing and investigations.
- Work with an outside law firm to handle claims.
- Impose on outside counsel revised billing requirements that reduce per-matter legal expenses.
- Improve efficiency within risk management and the Legal Department by updated computerizing case management and document production.
- Prevention: educate company personnel regarding the United States' product liability and safety-related concerns, and avoidance through quality control standards pertaining to design, manufacturing, and product warnings.

As you can see above, companies need not only specific objectives to evaluate risks but also specific processes on how to achieve such objectives. Both are necessary when evaluating risk assessments, especially when dealing with LRM issues.

7

Conducting Legal Risk Assessment

Form: LRM Investigation

Risk assessments are conducted in phases, once a risk assessment plan is established pursuant to the risk assessment evaluation. The normal risk assessment phase consists of the five major phases of the enterprise risk management (ERM) model. Such ERM based is an excellent example of the phases needed for a total LRM solution such as:

TOTAL LRM SOLUTION

Phase 1	Risk assessment project plan
Phase 2	Identification of risk through workshops and interviews
Phase 3	Risk scoring—scoring the probability of risk
Phase 4	Critical risk analysis
Phase 5	Implementation of action plan

Let's look at each phase in more detail:

7.1 Phases

Phase 1: Identification

In phase 1, the company needs to decide which divisions or departments need a legal risk assessment or risk review. Normally the most critical divisions or departments should be looked at first, such as Service, HR, Sales, and any other department or division in which lawsuits or claims either arise or can be initiated. Normally, the divisions with most contact with employees or the public should be reviewed first. Departments with the most contact with the public equals the highest risk.

Once a division is picked, the company risk manager or Risk Management Department should do an initial risk assessment to determine what major areas of risk or what legal issues stand out. If you are dealing with the Service Department, perhaps claims or response times are a major issue. Once identified, phase 2 must be implemented—the risk identification/awareness phase. In this phase, the major areas of risk are identified and made known to the stakeholders. The process of phase 2 is conducted by using various tools as set forth below.

Phase 2: The process

- Risk identification and awareness phase

In conducting departmental risk assessments, a core process tool to use would normally be interviews as well as document review. An example would be:

- Conduct interviews of key departments.
- Review of processes and procedures
- Review of documents

- Identify critical risk factors through surveys.
- Prioritize critical risk factors.
- Develop action plans.

7.1.1 Interviews

- Why use confidential interviews as a tool to identify legal risk?

I have found that the use of confidential employee interviews is one of the most effective ways of identifying legal risk. This is because employees may not only need certain internal corporate processes and procedures explained to them in order to evaluate the probability of risk or legal risk, but confidentiality is usually needed in order for employees to really open up and talk to management about issues and concerns. Remember, when conducting a risk assessment of any department within the company, the Risk Management Department or Law Department must not only try to identify the risks but must also find out why the risks exist and how to mitigate or resolve them. Feedback from employees is essential when trying to identify and resolve legal risk.

A good question to ask during a legal risk assessment identification phase would be:

- What are the major risks in any department that could or would generate legal liability or negatively impact the brand of the company?

So it is advised to use a number of tools—interviews, workshops, surveys, document reviews, industry information, or even focus groups—to identify risk as well as decide how to respond. Once the legal risks are identified, it is easier to decide how to address such risks, whether through training, workshops, new processes, etc.

7.1.2 Other Phases

In phase 2 of the risk assessment, it is important to identify categories of risk, which may also identify the kinds of risk and their severity. Such categories may be:

- Strategic
- Operational
- Financial
- Human Resources
- Technology
- Legal and regulatory

By looking at the categories of risk and identifying the major areas of risk, it is easier to manage the risk and come up with solutions. Perhaps the risks consist of weak internal controls or an absence of protocols or systems when dealing with the public or even a failure to appreciate a country's labor laws or governmental regulations.

Phase 3: Use of risk tools will obviously help to identify the probability of risk and severity of the risk. Each business unit may want to develop tools to identify the risk and its severity within its own unit.

Phase 4: Once phase 3 is accomplished and the risk scoring tool is used to determine the probability and severity of such risk, a critical risk analysis must be conducted using risk models. Such a critical risk analysis can then be used to formulate an action plan, as in phase 5

Phase 5: The most important phase of a legal risk assessment is the implementation of an action plan. It can consist of training, audits, enforcing existing processes, and developing new processes and tools, as well as other procedures. It is the action plan that will if properly implemented mitigate the legal risk a company faces.

8

General Product Liability Considerations and Risk Management

Suggested forms and policies to implement appropriate product liability safeguards include:

Form: Claims Defense Policy
Form: Product Loss Control Policy
Form: Product Loss Control Committee
Form: Claims Investigation and Procedure

For more on loss control, see Appendix A.

8.1   Product Liability Concerns and Costs

Product liability claims, product recall cases, and related litigation, besides hurting the company's brand, image, and reputation, will entail many costs, expenses, and legal fees such as:

- Costs related to product incidents, including recall, retrofit, management and employee time, and lost profits
- Legal costs, including litigation costs
- Increased insurance costs

- Costs including those associated with a loss control program and other risk management–related processes

In order to implement a risk management program that covers all legal issues related to product liability in a specific jurisdiction or country, an analysis of the legal theories related to product liability in that jurisdiction or country should be reviewed. In the United States, such legal theories include:

8.1.1 Typical Legal Theories on which a Plaintiff May Base a Product Liability Claim and/or Class Action

- Breach of express warranty
  - Express warranty can be created by:
    - "Affirmation of fact or promise" made by the seller to the buyer, which relates to the product and becomes part of the basis of the bargain
    - Advertisements, labels, literature, samples or models, catalogues, and brochures
- Breach of implied warranty
  - Implied warranty of merchantability is implied by law in every contract with a merchant for the sale of goods—a guarantee that product will be merchantable (of commercially acceptable quality).
  - Implied warranty of fitness for particular purpose arises when the seller has reason to know that buyer wants goods for a particular purpose and buyer is relying on seller's skill to select suitable goods.
- Negligence

A manufacturer of goods or products has a duty to use reasonable care in the design of goods so as to protect those who will use them from an unreasonable risk of harm while the goods are being used. This includes using the goods for their intended purpose, or for any purpose, which could reasonably be expected.

This duty extends to unintended yet reasonably foreseeable uses, as well as intended uses of the goods or products.

- Strict liability

In the United States, the Restatement of Torts Section 402 sets forth the special liability of the seller of a product in a defective condition resulting in physical harm to the consumer.

- 402A. Special Liability of Seller of Product in a defective condition unreasonably dangerous to the user or consumer or to his property is subject to liability for physical harm thereby caused to the ultimate user or consumer, or to his property, if the seller is engaged in the business of selling such a product, and it is expected to and does reach the user or consumer without substantial change in the condition in which it is sold.[1]
- Deceptive and unfair trade practices (DUTP)
  - In the United States, every state has a statue prohibiting deceptive trade practices.
  - DUTP claims are not based on contract; contractual limitations on liability, therefore, do not apply.
  - Claims are not based on warranty, so disclaimers of warranty do not apply.
  - DUTP can include:
    - Failure to disclose information
    - Oral and written misrepresentations
    - Ambiguous representations
    - Breach of warranty obligations
- U.S. consumer class actions against manufacturers

---

[1]   Restatement of Torts (Second), Section 402, 1964.

These class actions are normally brought in the United States on the following basis:

- DUTP claims
  - Aggregation of numerous small claims
  - Simplified compliance with states' procedural requirements
  - Proof of deceptive practices by defendant's documents (e.g., advertising literature)
  - Common deceptive practice to all class numbers
  - Common product defect
- Regulatory and general legal considerations
  - Consumer Product Safety Commission (CPSC)
    - CPSA Section 15(b) Reports: "Every manufacturer of a consumer product distributed in commerce, and every distributor and retailer of such product, who obtains information which reasonably supports the conclusion that such product . . . _(2) contains a defect which could create a substantial product hazard described in Subsection (A)(2) or (3) creates an unreasonable risk of serious injury or death, shall immediately inform the commission unless the manufacturer . . . has actual knowledge that the commission has been adequately informed of such defect, failure to comply, or such risk . . ."[2]

8.2   Sources of Product Liability Risk

There are a number of areas that a company's Risk Management Department (RMD) or related divisions must consider when implementing a comprehensive legal risk management program to address product liability concerns. The main concerns are sources of risk, whether departmental or process oriented. Each step of

---

[2]   CPSA, 15 U.S.C. Sec 2064(b).

the design, manufacturing, sales, and distribution chain contains numerous risks, including:

8.2.1 *Potential Sources of Product Liability*

- Product design
  - Performance specifications
  - Safety analysis and features
  - Labeling
  - Instructions for use
  - Warnings and cautions
  - Detectability of malfunctions
  - Serviceability
  - Product warranty
- Manufacturing and distribution
  - Manufactured to specifications
  - Components meet design specification
  - Product testing
  - Product packaging
  - Record-keeping procedures
  - Suppliers
  - Contractors
  - "OEM" or "VAR" customers
  - Distributors
- Product promotion and service
  - Advertising copy
  - Product literature
  - Marketing and promotional material
  - Service and repair procedures

8.3 Possible Defenses to Product Liability Exposure

Though consumer warranties in the United States are governed for the most part under the Magnuson-Moss Act, the Uniform Commercial Code (UCC) addresses warranties when used in the sale of goods in the U.S. The proactive use of warranties can be seen as another tool to limit product liability exposure when dealing with the sale of goods in the United States. Such defenses include:

- Breach of express warranty
  - Possible defenses to a breach of express warranty claim include:
    - Lack of causation
    - Lack of damages
    - Disclaimers: UCC §2-316 provides that a disclaimer will be effective only to the extent that it can be read consistently with any express warranties made.
- Assumption of risk: UCC §2-715 indicates that when the plaintiff assumes the risk by using a product while aware of the breach of warranty, any resulting injuries are not proximately caused by the breach.
- Contributory negligence: Courts in contributory negligence jurisdictions have adopted an approach similar to that used in strict liability in tort—that unreasonable failure to discover the defect does not bar recovery, but that unreasonable conduct after discovery does bar recovery.
- Breach of implied warranty
  - Possible defenses to a breach of implied warranties claim:
    - Assumption of risk: UCC §2-715 indicates that when the plaintiff assumes the risk by using a product while aware of the breach of warranty, any resulting injuries are not proximately caused by the breach.
    - Contributory negligence: Courts in contributory negligence jurisdictions have adopted an approach similar to that used in strict liability in tort—that unreasonable failure to discover the defect does not bar recovery, but that unreasonable conduct after discovery does bar recovery.

- Comparative negligence: Courts in comparative negligence jurisdictions use comparative fault notions in warranty cases to reduce damage awards in the same way as in strict liability cases.
- Disclaimer: Disclaimers of liability for breach of implied warranty must be specific and are narrowly construed. See UCC §2-316.
- Notice of breach: UCC §2-607 requires the buyer to give the seller notice within a reasonable time after the buyer discovers or should have discovered the breach.
- Lack of (horizontal) privity: The implied warranties most likely will extend only to the immediate buyer and his or her family and not to third parties such as those parties which receive the products as gifts or buy them used.
- Statute of limitations.

8.4 Loss Control

Loss control is another tool a company or organization should use to minimize or reduce risk. If properly used, loss control can reduce losses and decrease exposure associated with such losses. Harrington and Niehaus define loss control simply as "efforts that reduce expected losses".[3] Loss control refers to those processes that can prevent, reduce, or mitigate losses. Loss control processes, in other words, if properly used, can mitigate and reduce risk. Normally, loss control processes can be very effective in reducing product liability costs and expenses.

---

[3] Harrington and Niehaus, Risk Management and Insurance, 2nd edition, New York:McGraw Hill, 2003

8.4.1   *Loss Control: Possible Defenses to Product Liability Exposure*

Loss control processes are usually divided into two main categories—loss prevention and loss reduction. They are defined as follows:[4]

- Loss prevention: activities that reduce expected losses of inventory or monies associated with inventory by proactively reducing the frequency of losses
- Loss reduction: activities that reduce expected losses of inventory or monies associated with inventory by decreasing the size of the loss, which is a reactive and not a proactive process

8.4.2   *Loss Control Committee*

Implementation of loss control processes, whether loss reduction or prevention, is best managed by oversight of a loss control committee or LCC. The loss control committee, consisting of members from Sales and Marketing, Legal, Risk Management, and Service (as well as others if needed) can review current practices, policies, and procedures to make informed decisions as to the viability of loss control policies. The loss control committee can review warranties, labels, literature, and related product literature to make recommendations that could prevent claims by preventing losses.

I found the loss control committee to be a very useful tool if used properly and on a regular basis. Though information provided to and considered by the loss control committee may be limited in scope, the reasonable judgment of people with various viewpoints from various departments within a company can often prove to be very valuable, especially when given as a group after careful consideration.

---

[4] Id

For a sample loss control policy and loss control committee form, see Appendix A.

8.4.3 Loss Control: Case in Point

Sarah Jones, the risk manager for XYZ Company, was excited about her new duties. Because of rising product claims and increasing reports of product malfunctions in the field, the VP of Service persuaded management to establish the Product Loss Control Committee (PLCC), with Sarah as the RLCC lead.

Sarah, however, was not exactly certain who should be on the committee and what the committee's mandate was. She decided to focus on product issues, thinking that product safety, R&D, quality control, and claims handling were all important aspects to be considered by the PLCC. Sarah knew, however, that before she could do anything she needed the express approval of executive management. She therefore decided to create a policy and procedures manual, which would be approved by the CEO and VP of Service.

Working with her internal Law Department, Sarah developed a policy and procedures manual setting forth the duties and responsibilities of the PLCC in detail. Under the PLCC policy and procedures manual, the company's various division VPs were responsible for the development and maintenance of the PLCC and had to appoint a representative of each division to sit on the PLCC. Furthermore, the PLCC policy and procedures manual set forth all processes and procedures regarding complaints and claim handling as well as claim processing.

While talking to XYZ's insurance company, Sarah mentioned the establishment of the PLCC to the lead insurance agent, Mr. Smith.

Mr. Smith was intrigued, stating a proper PLCC would held decrease XYZ's insurance premiums, as a loss control process was considered a very valuable risk management tool and often led to processes that would help control product loss and claims and expenses associated with products. Mr. Smith asked for more details regarding the PLCC.

- What processes and procedures should Sarah consider for the PLCC?
- How should claims handling be addressed?
- Should the PLCC consider product warranty issues?
- Should the PLCC review product literature?
- Should the PLCC consider claims defense processes?
- Who should be on the PLCC for it to be an effective loss control process?

9

New Product Planning and Development Management

New product planning and development has the potential for great risk, but also for mitigation of risk if the right mechanisms can be used in a timely fashion. As stated previously, companies need to be very detailed to avoid product liability litigation and legal exposure. If implemented in a timely and correct manner, such processes can minimize legal risk, especially regarding class actions.

9.1   Stages

Product development and planning normally involves four distinct stages prior to mass production:

- Product planning
- Development planning
- Development (implementation)
- Production readiness

In each stage there is potential cause for risk, as each stage involves processes that can potentially expose a manufacturing company to great legal risk such as:

- Product planning
  - Product planning & review
  - Design
  - User interface development
- Development planning and standardization
  - Standardization of design
  - Development of machine parts
  - Development of electric parts
  - Software development
  - Tooling development
  - Engineering sample
  - Final parts development
- Development implementation
  - User manual and training manual developed
  - Regulations reviewed and approval obtained
  - Reliability assurance test performed
  - Final user interface developed
  - Product preparation for mass production
- Production readiness
  - Test reliability of mass production
  - Create manufacturing training material
  - Prepare JIGs and dyes

In each stage of product design, development, and production, many departments must share and coordinate information, tasks, roles and responsibilities, and communication with each other. Failure to do so in an effective manner in accordance with proper procedures and processes leads to not only failure but potential legal liability. For instance, let's look at the main stages of a product planning cycle in a new product development scenario.

9.2 Product Planning

A typical product planning life cycle would involve at least eight departments and look something like this:

- Product planning department
  - Conceptualize product development
  - Establish management plan for product
  - Share information between related departments
- Marketing
  - Confirm long- and short-term marketing strategy of product
  - Suggest retail sales points
  - Project potential sales issues
  - Strategize marketing launch
  - Plan advertising for launch
- R&D
  - Suggest development of technology and parts
  - Suggest new features
  - Review development plan in accordance with product's features
- Design department
  - Review strategy
  - Suggest materials, design, and colors of parts and products
  - Research and analyze design trends
- Quality control
  - Provide appropriate standards and regulations
  - Review production liability laws
  - Supply quality checklist
  - Review field claims at product issue
- Technology planning
  - Analyze long- and short-term trend and forecast of future technologies
- Others
  - Collect information from end-user
  - Share service information
  - Review information from sellers, distributors, and dealers

9.3 Standardization

One of the key stages of new product development once product planning is finalized is development planning and standardization. This stage involves many processes that, if not handled properly, involve legal risk. A typical "standardization" stage would look something like this:

- R&D Department
  - Construct product structure
  - Covert product design into engineering sample
  - Standardize all parts
  - Confirm engineering samples
- Quality Department
  - Provide past failure examples and improvements
  - Provide quality control information
  - Review designs
- Production Technology Department
  - Establish pre-mass-production line
  - Create concept design for production line
  - Provide advice on improvements
- Design Department
  - Materialize design concept through 3D modeling or mock-up
  - Cooperate with Marketing Department
- Product Planning Department
  - Review design in regard to product planning
- Marketing Department
  - Review designs in regard to marketing
- Legal Department
  - Research existing patents
  - Apply for patents
  - Review designs

9.4 Development Implementation (Including Design Verification and Production Validation)

- R&D
  - Product evaluation review
  - Preparation of parts development
  - Provide parts for working sample
- Production technology
  - Design manufacturing process
- Quality control
  - Establish quality standards
    - Testing of parts
    - Testing of specs
- Design
  - Check structural specs
- Marketing
  - Review marketing and promotional material

9.5 Production Readiness

The last stage before mass production involves the same of the most important processes as regarding legal risk. This is the last stage prior to putting a product into the stream of commerce.

- Production technology
  - Lead mass production line
  - Optimize manufacturing
  - Design mass production flow structure
- Quality control
  - Test reliability of mass production
  - Review mass production product quality
- Product planning
  - Check on product feature charges
  - Check on design feature charges
- Marketing
  - Check on product launch

- Review production quality
- Provide market info
- Other departments
  - Provide end-user manual
  - Provide service training manual
  - Provide quality check manual

9.6 Mitigating Legal Risk in New Product Development and Planning

When it comes to legal risk, a company must take the production of new products seriously. A company faces various threats, especially class action exposure in the United States. Such exposure comes from claims involving:

- Breach of warranty
- Deceptive and unfair trade laws (DUPTA)
- Product defect claims

LRM processes can be used to minimize legal risk, especially those involving class action claims, if properly implemented. They include the following processes:

9.6.1 *Limitation of Remedies*

A company may limit remedies that end users have through properly drafted warranties. In the United States, the Magnuson-Moss Warranty Act limits remedies to whichever the warrantor elects:

- Refund
- Repair
- Replacement

A properly drafted warranty can limit the end users' remedy. Also, it can limit the liability from a buyer or consumer's failure to comply with conditions for warranty coverage. By using the buyer's own conduct as a basis of an affirmative defense, manufacturers can limit their liability.

So the first step in minimizing your liability or minimizing legal exposure from the sale of goods or products is the use of an appropriate warranty, which limits remedies and limits or eliminates warranties based on the buyer's failure to comply with conditions of warranty coverage.

9.6.2 Warnings

Another useful LRM tool to minimize liability is to develop appropriate warnings in product literature.

Such warnings should:

- Describe product's limitation.
- Describe product risks.
- Stress dangers of not following the instructions.
- Warn of misuse and hazards to the user.
- Specify maintenance procedures of the product.
- Ensure that labels and warnings comply with federal and industry regulations and standards.

9.6.3 Sales and Marketing Literature

In order to protect itself from class actions involving the sale of products, a company should also review its sales and marketing literature.

- Do all sales and advertising manuals accurately describe the product?
- Are all disclaimers and limitations of warranties adequately reflected in the sales literature?
- Does the sales literature contain misleading statements?

9.6.4 *Other Ways to Limit Liability*

There are other processes and procedures and LRM tools to use to limit liability. Some will be described elsewhere in this book. However, some of the more common ones depend on following detailed product planning processes set forth in this chapter, including:

- Early detection of defective products
- Use of processes to carefully select vendors involved in manufacturing
  - Do they have insurance?
  - Can they indemnify you?
- Implementation of a loss control policy procedure
- Use of insurance coverage

The LRM processes outlined in this chapter involve design, warnings, warranties, labels, and service procedures that can effectively limit or mitigate legal liability. They are set forth in more detail in the next chapter.

10

Design Risk Management

When designing products, manufacturing companies need to be very detailed to avoid product liability litigation in the United States. Product planning is a very detailed process involving many departments, as we have seen. As part of an overall plan to reduce risks of product liability litigation as well as class actions and government investigations raised by CPSC or FTC concerns, it is recommended manufacturing companies develop a detailed design risk program or "DRP." Such processes can minimize, reduce, or prevent liability when claims are brought. A checklist should be developed to cover such issues. Checklists are another handy tool to use when looking at processes and procedures to minimize legal liability. Product planning and design process considerations of an effective DRP should normally include the following:

10.1 Product Design Issues and Considerations[1]

- Written procedures for the design program, including:

---

[1] For a discussion see Kenneth Ross, Martin Foley and Barbara Wrubel, Product Liability of Manufacturers, Preventions and Defense, NY: Practicing Law Institute, 1988

- Design choices—consideration of alternative designs
- Specifications—definition of specifications used in designing the product
- Establishment of a design review committee
- Establishment of written procedures for the development of specifications, which verify that specifications are accurately reflected in the designs.
- Establishment of procedures for construction and testing and prototypes.
- During the design: Evaluation and consideration of:
  - Determine types of people likely to be exposed to the product, consider unique risks to these groups
  - Tailor labeling and develop safety features to address the unique risks to the intended users
  - Risks of intended use—test and evaluate to determine what risks are presented if the product is used as intended; reduce these risks through design changes, safety features, and/or labeling.
- Assess the likelihood that products will be misused; identify and reduce the probability of misuse through design features, safety features, and/or labeling.
- Malfunction: Incorporate features that prevent critical failure or malfunction. Is it safe to use? If not, what features can render it safe?
- Design manufacturing considerations: Can the product be manufactured in accordance with the specifications?
- Serviceability: Are the products difficult to service or maintain correctly?
- Consider the materials, components, equipment, and software that should be used in manufacturing the device.
- Assure that designs comply with applicable code certifications and standards. Are they appropriate? Do they comply with governmental and industry standards?
- If using an outside company to develop or provide product designs, review and evaluate the designs.

- Monitoring of designs, including continued research and testing and review of new information respecting the products.
- Record-keeping of all product designs and processes to show all the above processes were considered.
- Is everyone in the design department familiar with all design procedures and processes?

10.2 Labeling

Proper labeling is also mandatory to avoid or mitigate legal risk or exposure. Numerous class actions have and are continuing to be brought on the basis that product labels were misleading, false, or failed to adequately warn of the danger posed by the product. Such labels need not only to warn the users against all risks, including those risks that are obvious, but the labels must clearly state hazards and warn anyone about the potential or likely consequences of using the product improperly. Failure to do so will result in litigation. Of course, labels need to follow the requisite local standards.

It is recommended that significant time be spent on labels, as improper use of a product resulting in injury may very well end up in litigation. Labels may not play a big role in determining potential liability but inadequate labels or labels that fail to follow local rules and regulations can result in governmental fines, penalties or worse.

The following checklist summarizes what companies need to do when considering labels.

10.2.1 Labels, Labels, Labels

- It is important to establish a labeling review committee. Manufacturers need to review and modify labels on a regular basis, so it is advised that a committee be formed to handle it. Or, in fact, the loss control committee can help in this regard. I have used the loss control committee to review labels as well as using a labeling review committee. A regular review is necessary to keep the labels updated which is quite important to prevent and minimize product liability.

- Consider the intended users of the product. How should the label or labels be drafted?
  - If general consumers will be using the product, develop labeling that is easy to read and understand, warn against all risks, including all obvious risks, and warn about the consequences of improper use.
  - If professional operators will be using the product, you should specify on the labeling that only qualified personnel may use/operate the device and warn against unapproved uses.
- Provide users with clear and concise directions, information, and precaution for use on labels, if possible. Of course, it should also be reflected in the manuals and instructions.
- Ensure that the label is accurate, complete, visible, and easily understood by the intended users.
- Provide information on labels affixed to the product or through inserts or packaging.
- When it is not feasible to provide full information on a label affixed to the product, affix a label that refers users to inserts or handbooks that will provide full information.
- Warnings and information on the label should be consistent with warnings and information used elsewhere, such as in packaging or inserts. You do not want the label to contradict or modify warnings made elsewhere.
- Include information on where and how to obtain service and warn against improper or unauthorized service.
- Include information on where users should send complaints about the products; encourage users and distributors to report adverse information.
- Include adequate warnings in labeling, including warnings as to:
  - Risks of customary use

- Risks of misuse and unapproved uses
- Risks of improper maintenance
- Include information in labeling on:
  - Maintenance
  - Service
  - Alterations
  - Where to send complaints or questions
- Review all inserts and information on packaging for accuracy and to assure that they are consistent with other labeling elsewhere.
- Comply with all appropriate governmental requirements or regulations. If selling products in other countries, your labels should also comply with the labeling requirements of those countries or local jurisdictions in which your products are sold. This is another process that is quite important and must be followed.

10.2.2 Post sale Monitoring of Labels

Once the product is sold in the marketplace, it is best to follow up on the adequacy of labels. Reports from Service might provide some insight, as the Service Department usually hears about defects, misuse, and other performance related problems first.

- A company should monitor the adequacy and accuracy of labels.
- A company should establish a field service reporting mechanism to a committee such as the loss control committee on how devices are used in the field and to give information on service and maintenance problems caused by users who misunderstand the labels.
- A company should evaluate complaints, failures, and malfunctions as it relates to labels.
- It is advised that a company evaluate all failures and malfunctions to determine whether they were caused by poor labeling or by user misunderstanding of the labeling.

- It is important to monitor labeling practices in the industry. What are they?
- A company should also monitor legal and regulatory developments related to labeling.
- A manufacturer should also keep labeling-history files, including test results and records of post market surveillance, as well as loss-prevention procedures. These files will be necessary in the event of a product liability lawsuit to show the requisite steps were taken to prevent injury or that the manufacturer took all possible steps to prevent injury.

10.3 Marketing Literature and Review of Manuals

Not only does product design and labels play a part in a good legal risk management program or LRM program, but a good LRM program requires manufacturers and distributors to review all marketing literature as well. Often companies fail to adequately review marketing literature even though poorly drafted marketing literature results in claims, litigation, and class actions, especially if a user is injured when allegedly following or relying on statements made in product literature. Plaintiff lawyers often cite misleading marketing literature as a major reason for filing DUTP claims. It is extremely important that a company invests time and resources to ensure its marketing literature is correct. This process may determine if a company or organization is exposed to class actions or not. Therefore, it is advised that a company should take the following important steps when drafting and reviewing marketing literature.

10.3.1 Marketing and Advertising Literature

- Review all published statements about the products, including marketing, advertising, product listings, and catalogues to ensure that they do not mislead users or encourage users to disregard directions and warnings contained in the labeling.

- Include provisions in distribution and purchasing agreements so that distributors and/or end users will:
    - Notify the company of any product failures or malfunctions or potential or alleged malfunctions.
    - Use the products strictly in accordance with the instructions provided.
    - Refrain from using the product after failure of the product or after a product malfunction.
    - Use the product only with compatible systems, components, or parts. Many products these days are used in conjunction with other products or systems, such as those sold by VARs.
    - Have the product serviced only by company service personnel or entities approved or certified by the company and avoid using unauthorized service providers.
    - Keep and provide the company with records of product sales for traceability purposes, especially if the product is manufactured in lots or batches. This will be important in the event of a product recall.
- Traceability: Provide for the tracing of products and important components to the point of origin by identifying and marking products during manufacture. Keep and maintain records of product lot and serial numbers, product release information, and identity of product users. This is vital in case of defective products that can be traced to a specific lot, which is necessary during a product recall.
- Warn against combining your products with incompatible systems. You never know what buyers or end users will do regarding your product. Even VARS or distributors may try and combine your products with incompatible systems. You should also prohibit VARS and distributors from combining your products with incompatible systems in your contract with them.

10.3.2 Establish a Review Committee to Review Manuals, Labels, and Warnings

I established a review committee to draft and review manuals, warnings, and labels. This was very effective, as not only the Sales and Marketing Departments had input but obviously Service, Legal, and Risk, as well. In fact, the loss control committee can provide this function or can provide assistance in forming a review committee. The more input from the various relevant departments the better.

- Instruction manuals[2]
  - In general, instruction manuals or guidebooks should contain detailed information not only about the product in question but also about publication of the manual and a disclaimer of relevant warranties, if applicable, including the date of publication and a description of the manual(s) as well as; (i) disclaimers of express or implied warranties, if needed; (ii) the name and description of the product and its overall function and other relevant product information, such as its model, lot, or serial number; a summary at the front of the manual, directing attention to any known product hazards, if any; (iii) consistent restatements of all warnings that appear on the products and additional safety information; (iv) a statement of the recommended operational limits of the product, accompanied by warnings against foreseeable misuses or mistreatment of the product(s); (v) a listing of the relevant codes or standards or service classifications that it complies with; (vi) a detailed listing of the location and function of all

---

[2] For a good discussion on drafting instruction manuals and warnings see Kenneth Ross, Martin Foley and Barbara Wrubel, *Product Liability of Manufacturers, Preventions and Defense,* New York: Practicing Law Institute,1988

components, parts, and accessories; (vii) instructions for assembly (especially complex products that may require separate manuals for each product-Related task-installation, maintenance, repair, etc;(viii) installation instructions; directions for operation if needed; directions for inspection, maintenance, and adjustment of the product(s); (ix) instruction for overhaul and repair of the product(s) if needed; instructions as to when special training or other qualifications may be required to perform a given task or operation with regards to the operation of the product(s); and (x) instruction for safe disposal of the product(s) or components thereof;

- Information on how to obtain additional or replacement manuals; and information on reordering parts, emphasizing safety-critical items, as well as information on obtaining replacements for warning labels.

10.3.3 Review Warnings[3]

A great deal of time should be spent to ensure warnings are appropriate for the product being sold. It is very important. Therefore, the following steps are recommended:

- The warning must adequately indicate the scope of the danger.
- The warning must reasonably communicate the extent of seriousness of the harm that could result from misuse of the product.
- The physical aspects of the warning must be adequate to alert a reasonably prudent person to the danger.
- The warning must indicate the consequences that might result from failure to follow it.

---

[3] Ibid

- The means to convey the warning must be adequate to bring the warning home to the user.
- The specific nature of the hazard and the gravity of the risk to which users may be exposed must be clearly stated in a warning.
- Indicate the level of hazard seriousness.
- Indicate the likelihood of the hazard resulting in harm.
- Note: Inadequate warnings have been the subject of much litigation in the United States. It is vital to have correct warnings on your product as well as in the instruction manual. Also, other countries besides the U.S. may take warnings seriously. It is advisable to discuss warnings with local legal counsel and check what local regulations exist, if any, that will impact the warnings you use.

10.4 Manufacturing and Distribution Issues

Obviously, when manufacturing a product, a company complies with local manufacturing standards. But, if it decides to sell and distribute products internationally, or if in the United States it decides to distribute such products interstate, what are its concerns? Companies selling interstate or internationally need to comply with all applicable manufacturing standards, including international standards, that are applicable to the relevant industry. Such standards may call for testing, certification, even certification of third-party service providers. You should make certain that your manufacturing processes are conducted in light of all regulatory requirements and that they address all legal issues. Therefore, applicable LRM processes regarding manufacturing should include the following consideration of manufacturing issues and warnings.

10.4.1 Manufacturing Issues

- Comply with all required manufacturing standards.
- Provide for different types of testing of devices, components, and material at different stages of the manufacturing process.

- Assure through testing that the manufactured device meets design and performance specifications.
- Conduct testing that accounts for the following:
  - Reliability
  - Environmental factors
  - System interface
  - Safety features
  - Serviceability
  - Shelf life and storage conditions

- Conduct validation of testing processes in accordance with applicable federal or international regulatory guidelines.
- Address quality of equipment used in manufacturing.
- Address quality of software.
- Address quality and suitability of buildings and facilities in which items are stored or manufactured.
- Procedures for testing of components and materials obtained from suppliers, and procedures for auditing suppliers and contractors.
- Agreements with suppliers and contractors, which include provisions that will help you address loss prevention concerns, including provisions for the following:
  - Periodic audits of suppliers
  - Notice to you of any significant malfunctions in the product supplied or manufactured

10.4.2 Service Issues and Procedures

Service processes and procedures, if correctly implemented, will not only mitigate legal risk and exposure but will actually first alert a company to any potential design or manufacturing defects as well as label, product manual, or literature issues. Service is usually the first division or department in contact with the end user or consumer. It is, in other words, the front line of a company's defense. It is the first to know if there is a problem. Therefore, it is recommended the following processes be strictly implemented and followed by the Service Department:

10.4.3 Service

- Investigations: It is vital that Service evaluate all service-related complaints according to written procedures that set forth valid and uniform criteria to determine validity, seriousness, fault, and repeatability, and determine whether the complaint falls within government regulatory requirements.
- Provide new information on proper use of risks associated with use.
- Warn against further use of an obsolete or hazardous product.
- Warn against misuse or unapproved use and supply information on the risks of such use.
- Advise when the product should be repaired or replaced.
- Provide information about obtaining product service from the manufacturer.
- Provide information about where to obtain service from third parties if necessary.
- Train field-service personnel in loss-prevention concerns, including the potential liability impact of their statements to users. Service personnel are often the first people users come into contract with and misstatements can lead to litigation or claims.
- Require field-service personnel to submit standard forms giving information on product problems and contacts with users.
- Instruct field-service personnel who also service other companies' products to:
  - Repair only products about which they have sufficient information.
  - Disclaim responsibility for the inherent quality of other companies' products.

- Notify other companies of any problems relating to their products.
- Warn users to have products only serviced and repaired by authorized personnel.
- Document product-service loss-prevention measures, and keep records of employee training and relevant agreements with users and service companies.

10.4.4 *Third-Party Service Providers*

It is common for manufacturers, especially in the consumer products industry, to use third-party service providers to provide service, especially product repair. Many foreign manufacturers do not have the resources or facilities in all countries to provide direct service without using third-party service providers. This is especially true in the consumer electronic industry. The use of third-party service providers, of course, inserts a third party in between the manufacturer, distributor or dealer, and the end user or consumer. It can be another source of legal risk! Therefore, the following processes should be required of third-party service providers:

- A report from the third-party service provider should include information such as:
  - Information on the product repaired
  - The nature of the work performed
  - The equipment and materials used to repair the product, if any
  - The identity of user and service
  - The place and date of repair
  - The condition of the product as received
  - The testing performed
  - Information about their procedures, employee training, and quality assurance
  - Indemnification for liability created by improper servicing of the service-provider

- Written procedures for the certification of third-party service provider should be required. The company should audit the third-party service provider to determine compliance with procedures on a regular basis.

11

Risk Insurance

Insurance, if used properly, is a great tool to shift legal risk or exposure to another entity (i.e., the insurance provider). Many companies fail to adequately consider insurance options, cover risk, or consider appropriate insurance tools that can shift or transfer risk of loss, litigation, or claims. A proper legal risk management program needs to adequately address these issues and to consider the insurability of risk. Insurance, if properly used, can be a great LRM tool. It all starts with a risk assessment such as set forth below.

11.1 Insurance Considerations: Risk Assessment

- Conduct a risk assessment to create a business risk profile to identify factors that have the greatest financial impact, then integrate appropriate risk transfer strategies to stabilize insurance costs, mitigate extraordinary financial impact, ensure cost effective protection against catastrophic losses, leverage risk bearing capital, and optimize tax and accounting issues.
- Conduct an analysis of current coverage, amounts, deductibles, and excess.

- Consider custom-designed protection programs by product line (e.g., televisions, automobiles, or microwave ovens).
- Evaluate product recall insurance. Is it necessary?
- Investigate establishment of a captive insurance company.

11.1.1 Historical Data

It should be noted that companies use insurance as a risk mitigation or transfer tool and that they manage insurance programs differently than the average consumer. When developing a risk assessment of insurance considerations, data is extremely important when considering a probability or a risk-related event. The collection of relevant data will determine what kind of insurance policies can be obtained, the price, and even the availability of certain insurance programs. How far back a company can go historically to obtain data determines the potential risks a company faces and, therefore, what insurance program and provider is available as well as the costs involved.

When looking at risk insurance programs, the first question that should be asked by the company is whether it has accurate data. Does it have a good risk management information system in place? If not, does its insurance broker or provider have one? Or maybe the insurance broker or provider can help develop one.

Accurate data leads to the right risk management strategy and the right insurance program. Lack of data makes it harder to have an accurate picture as to the risks involved and, therefore, harder to develop the appropriate insurance strategy and program. It is necessary to obtain accurate historical data if at all possible.

11.2 Coverage

The main reason that companies make extensive use of insurance coverage is to diversify and shift risk through use of business-related insurance. Insurance, if properly used and maintained can be a major risk management tool.

A major issue facing companies when trying to insure legal risk is the insurability of the risk. In essence, the cost of insuring the risk may be too great to justify the particular form of risk insurance. So when a risk assessment identifies a business risk, not only does the company need to determine if insurance coverage exists to cover the risk, but whether the cost of such insurance justifies its acquisition. Many manufacturing companies will not purchase product recall insurance or similar insurance because of its expense. Some manufacturing companies or organizations will not even purchase credit insurance because of its expense. Therefore, a company or corporation must pay attention to costs and consider methods to reduce the cost of insurance.

11.3 Costs

There are numerous factors in determining the cost and the desirability and practicality of various forms of risk insurance. However, the most important factors in determining cost of the insurance product normally include:

- The cost of the insurance policy or risk insurance product.
- Insurance premiums, if any.
- Whether coinsurance is required. Note: coinsurance is a specific portion of the loss (i.e., 10 percent, etc.) the insured is required to pay.
- Deductibles: this eliminates use of insurance for small claims as deductibles maybe too expensive or burdensome to pay in case a loss is a minor one.
- Contractual provisions placing specific burdens on the insured, such as exclusions to coverage.
- Policy limits: insurance policies usually limit the amount of coverage by placing a limit on the coverage. Perhaps the product liability coverage covers only $ 1 million per occurrence. The greater the policy limit, the more desirable the insurance policy is. However, it is always a function of cost.
- The claims history of the insured.

11.4 Insurance Analysis

A company, when deciding to shift its risk to an insurance company, must conduct a detailed analysis on potential insurance coverage as well as its own claims history or the potential claims in its industry, if it has no claims history. Only with an analysis of insurance coverage, deductibles, excess premiums, and coinsurance is it able to make a reasonable risk assessment as to the cost and desirability of the coverage. It is possible that such analysis may lend to customization of the insurance coverage (certain insurance programs may get different coverage) or certain forms of insurance coverage may not be purchased (i.e., product recall insurance) at all.

11.5 Evaluation of Insurance Providers

In determining which insurance provider to use for specific risks, a company needs to sit down with its insurance broker. Some companies opt to purchase insurance directly online or through agents or insurance company employees. However, it must be remembered that an insurance broker is an independent organization or entity that represents the purchaser of insurance, while an agent normally represents the insurance company.

Insurance brokers, which are usually brokers of record, normally have relationships with multiple insurers. As the broker of record, insurance brokers are normally able to obtain coverage quotes from numerous insurance companies. If a company seriously considers shifting risk through insurance, it needs to seriously consider those brokers that are able to provide risk management services and insurance products across a wide range of product lines and product categories. The large international brokers are often able to provide companies products and services that small or regional brokers are usually not able to provide. A company should take into consideration what insurance products and services it needs prior to sitting down with insurance brokers.

Though most companies use one broker of record, it is common for companies to contract with multiple insurers, as certain types of insurance coverage is very business specific. Thus, brokers tend to match the needs of the company to certain specific insurers, according to the industry or product line. For example, a company could have one insurance company handle EPL insurance, one handle credit insurance, one handle transportation or carrier related insurance, and another one handle product liability insurance.

It is advised, therefore, in order to develop a strong insurance program that adequately addresses the legal risks a company faces, the company must sit down with its broker after conducting a detailed risk assessment and analysis of current insurance coverage, amounts, deductibles, and excess. At a certain point a company may want to consider establishing a captive insurance company if the cost of insurance becomes too onerous.

11.6 Creating a Captive Insurance Company

What is a captive insurance company and why should it be considered? A captive insurance company is a closely held insurance company whose insurance business is primarily supplied and controlled by its owners. As the owners are the principal beneficiaries as the insured, they have direct involvement and influence over a captive's major operations.

Many companies, especially those who have subsidiaries, have opted to create a captive insurance company. Single parent captives, as they are sometimes called, are: (1) owned by a single entity, (2) exist primarily to underwrite risks of the parent and affiliated companies, (3) may also underwrite risks of unrelated parties, and (4) the financial results are normally consolidated with the parent's for financial reporting.

Besides single parent captives that underwrite the risks of the parent and its subsidiaries, there is also the group captive insurance company. Group captives (1) have multiple owners, (2) the owners are usually homogenous (they are in similar industries with similar risks), and (3) they engage in risk sharing, which is spelled out in corporate governance documents.

11.7 What Are the Primary Reasons to Consider a Captive Insurance Company?

- Primary reasons:
  - Cost
  - Coverage
  - Control

- Cost
  - Premiums that would ordinarily be paid to commercial insurers can be invested for the benefit of the captive, and the parent companies, until claims are paid.
  - Captives would expect lower "frictional" costs of providing coverage (i.e., lower acquisition cost and no imbedded shareholder profit to consider.

- Coverage
  - Greater flexibility: obviously the captive can provide greater coverage for the cost.
  - There are fewer limitations on ability to offer specific policy terms and conditions.
  - The insured can dictate terms as needed.
  - Result: better matches of needs and coverage.

- Control
Owners of a captive insurance company can exercise extensive direct control over all phases of the insurance process:

  - Underwriting
  - Claims adjusting and philosophy
  - Claims defense
  - Selection of counsel and philosophy
  - Selection of all vendors

- When should a captive insurance company be considered?

  Normally, when the company has:

  - consistently high insurance premiums in the commercial market,
  - uninsurable or difficult-to-place coverage,
  - decentralized business units with different insurance programs, and
  - a chance to take advantage of an arbitrage opportunity when reinsurance rates are considerably below rates of the commercial market.

- Risks

Like any insurance strategy, there are risks to consider. Such risks include:

- Laws governing captive insurance companies continue to evolve.
- Tax laws are transient and may change, affecting financial issued tied to taxation.
- Reinsurance market viability to the extent that reinsurance is used.
- Need for effective counseling on expected loss predictions, especially in early years.
- Exit issues—if members decide to return to commercial insurance, the captive may have created obligations that extend for several years.

- Other issues include:
  - Tax issues
  - Domicile—where to form the captive
    - Domestic
    - Offshore
  - Structure and loss sharing among owners

- Financial statement analysis
- Loss history analysis
- Comparison with alternatives
- Management: who will run the captive?

Note: the above issues should be considered during a feasibility study.

- So why is a captive insurance company worth considering?

There are many reasons to consider a captive insurance company, including:

- Problems with availability of commercial insurance.
- Financial opportunities to invest significant premium dollars for the company's benefit.
- When the company will benefit from lower-than-expected losses in given policy years, that will create a true incentive to produce safe and effective products and facilities.
- It could open greater reinsurance opportunities for the company.

- What should a company do when considering the captive insurance alternative?

- Conduct a feasibility analysis
- Review results of the analysis
- Agree on the data points involving the analysis
- Answer the above-mentioned issues

12

Credit Risk Management

Forms that may be useful in managing credit insurance and credit risk may include:

Form: Credit Risk Insurance
Form: Put Agreement

12.1 Credit Risk

Many companies that sell products to distributors, dealers, and retailers are exposed to credit risk when their customers don't pay for the product prior to or upon taking delivery of the product. This is often seen in purchase or sales contracts in which payment terms are net thirty, net forty-five, or net ninety. Of course, if the parties enter into a consignment arrangement, this is not the case.

Credit risk covers many loss scenarios in which a borrower (normally a buyer or customer) fails to fulfill its payment obligations. Such scenarios involve borrowers regardless of size or scope, including small companies, midsize, or even large companies, and sometimes even governments. Credit risk management is an extremely important piece in the LRM process. However, one of the most important forms of credit risk involves trade credit risk (i.e., the credit risk a company faces when its buyers or customers fail to pay on time or, in some situations, at all). How can a company handle its receivables credit risk or trade credit risk problems?

A company, when calculating the risk of nonpayment, needs to consider ways in which it can transfer or mitigate the risk.

12.2 Credit Risk Processes

Companies that experience credit risks on a regular basis should create a Credit Risk Department. The Credit Risk Department can implement a number of LRM processes or risk management tools and procedures that can mitigate or minimize the impact of credit risk. It is essential that a department or individual continuously monitors the credit risk of customers, as financial circumstances can change very quickly.

Normally, procedures and processes used by a Credit Risk Department in conjunction with Legal, Finance or Risk Management would include the following steps:

- Implementation of credit risk procedures: Normally standardized credit processes including credit terms and conditions of using the terms. The Credit Risk Department should run all terms by Legal. In fact the right terms on a credit application may in fact mitigate or minimize legal exposure that results from a customer's breach or default.
- Credit acceptance: Usually the first step in the process for credit approval where the company decides whether customers or buyers qualify for extended credit terms and if so under what terms. It is up to the Credit Risk Department in conjunction with Finance to decide what the payment terms would be, such as net thirty, net forty-five, or net sixty.
- Credit collection: Implementation of credit collection processes, including use of credit collection agencies.

- Use of credit risk insurance: Establishment and implementation of a credit risk insurance program to cover all or most customers on extended credit.

It should be noted that credit acceptance decisions are normally based on a number of factors, including:

- A company's credit history, if any
- The credit application form, if any
- A company's credit report or evidence of credit worthiness
- Financial statements of the company
- Corporate guarantees or cross corporate guarantees in case a company has subsidiaries or affiliates
- Standby letter of credit or some form of an L/C
- Personal guarantees of the principle shareholders if the organization or corporate entity is small
- Personal financial statements of partners or shareholders of the firm if it is small or medium size

12.3 Credit Risk Insurance

Commercial credit risk insurance, sometimes called "trade" credit risk insurance, can help a company protect its account receivables (A/R) from unexpected losses due to nonpayment or slow payment by the company's buyers. It usually covers nonpayment because of a buyer's insolvency but may also cover nonpayment due to political events that hinder payment or distributors on credit. A/R is the money owed to a company by its customer for products and services sold on credit. Normally, a sale is only treated as an account receivable after the customer has been invoiced for the product or service.

Depending on the industry and size of the company, it may or may not sell many or all of its products via credit. The risk, therefore, of nonpayment or slow payment (90 or 180 days after invoice, etc.) can be quite serious and expose the company to a potential crisis if the A/R is not paid. This is a major concern for any company selling its product(s) on credit.

12.3.1 Types of Credit Risks

Credit risk insurance normally covers two kinds of risk: commercial risk and political risk.

- Commercial risk:
- Insolvency or bankruptcy
- Protracted nonpayment
- Default of customer

Note: Credit risk insurance will not usually cover nonpayment due to contractual or legal disputes between the company and customer.

- Political risk:
- War, strikes or other potential civil disturbances
- Repatriation concerns: decision by the government not to allow repatriation or release of the funds
- Transfer risk: political events including wars or political disputes preventing transfer of payment

12.3.2 Benefits of Credit Insurance

There are numerous benefits for using credit insurance, if applicable. The most obvious benefits are:

- Transfer or mitigation of risk. Credit insurance assures a company that its A/R will be paid if one of its customers declares bankruptcy or is unable to pay. This is subject to the terms and conditions of the insurance policy.
- Improved cash flow. A timely collection of A/R provides much-needed operating cash flow.

- Sales. By using credit insurance, a company is able to extend more credit to its primary customers, promoting increased sales. This can be cyclical, allowing increased turnover of products and, therefore, increased sales.

12.3.3 Types of Coverage

Credit risk insurance normally consists of two kinds:

- Traditional coverage
- Excess-of-loss coverage

- Traditional coverage
  - It is cancelable by the insurer.
  - The insurer assigns credit limits and monitors specific credits.
  - Low deductibles.

- Excess-of-loss coverage
  - Non cancelable by insurer.
  - Policies usually provide a large discretionary credit limit.
  - Insured are able to set the majority of its credit limits on its customers.
  - Policy will include an annual aggregate deductible, above which losses are covered.

12.3.4 Insurance Provider

Credit insurance is a very specific insurance product. Usually, only international or specific insurance companies offer such insurance.

It should be noted that as credit risk covers many loss scenarios due to the failure of the borrower to fulfill payment obligations, trade credit risk encompasses the potential loss of a company's A/R due to nonpayment of a customer. Obviously, other credit risk scenarios exist, including project finance risks, but in this chapter we have concentrated on trade credit risk and trade credit risk insurance.

12.4 Put Agreements

Besides shifting or minimizing credit risk through insurance, companies are able sometimes to shift the risk of a buyer's nonpayment contractually. Put agreements, as they are called, may also protect a company's A/R when a purchaser fails to pay or is slow in paying its obligations. The terms of put agreements vary depending on which insurance provider, financial institution, or flooring company is willing to provide the put agreement. Normally, put agreements do not cover all receivables but will cover most of them. The put agreement can be used in conjunction with credit risk insurance if the credit risk insurance does not cover 100 percent of the risk.

12.5 Factoring

Another method of shifting or mitigating legal risk through insurance is through a factoring agreement. Basically, a company sells its A/R that is under a particular agreement to a financial institution or financial company that specializes in factoring agreements for a percentage of the A/R value. This works well if the company has a low-risk customer with poor cash flow. However, unlike put agreements, the factoring company will hold the company liable if the trade debt or outstanding A/R remains unpaid, such as in the case of bankruptcy of the debtor.[1]

---

[1] See Paul M Collier, *Fundamentals of Risk Management for Accountants and Managers*, Oxford, UK: Butterworth-Heinemann, Elsevier, 2009 p 181

13

Data Privacy and Risk Management

An often-overlooked area of risk management is data privacy or data protection. Many companies do not even associate data privacy with risk. However, as more and more countries begin to regulate the use of data by companies, data privacy has emerged as one of the hot topics of legal risk management. There are five main reasons why data privacy has become a major area of risk requiring attention of a company's Law Department, Risk Management Department and, ultimately, management itself.[1]

- Knowledge economy: Many businesses, through the use of the Internet and computers, compile and use large batches of data.
- Penalties: The European Union, Canada, and other countries, such as South Korea, have strict data privacy laws, which can levy significant penalties and fines for data privacy law violations.
- Publicity: As more and more people begin to jealously guard their personal data, a company's violation of data

---

[1] See the data privacy discussion set forth in chapter 24 of *International Corporate Practice*, edited by Carol Basri, New York: PLI, 2011, 24–2 ~ 24–3.

privacy laws can create a publicity nightmare, creating in effect a crisis of potential epic proportions. This has to be managed or contained.

- Extraterritorial reach: More and more data privacy laws restrict the transmission of data abroad, creating cross-border risks.
- Tougher regulations: More and more countries or jurisdictions, such as the European Union, are enacting tougher and tougher regulations on the use of personal data.

13.1 Personal Data

Though there are many kinds of data, data privacy issues normally concern "personal data." The European Union, for instance, considers personal data as any information that relates to an identifiable natural person. Such personal data can include an identification number, an employee's position, a person's e-mail address, phone number, etc. Basically, any information that relates to a natural person (not a corporation) regardless of whether the data relates to an employee or a customer, etc.[2]

The EU Data Directive, which is the European Union's comprehensive data privacy law, not only covers computerized data, but also covers written, Internet, and oral communications. Thus, any company doing business in Europe or interfacing with European companies that may result in the use of personal data from Europe could be exposed to a comprehensive data privacy law that is extraterritorial in reach.

Other countries may not have privacy laws as onerous as the European Union, such as the United States, but more and more countries are beginning to aggressively enforce their data privacy laws. This will only continue, especially as more lawsuits involving

---

[2] See Rebecca S Eisner, *European Union Data Privacy Requirements, A US Perspective, Tenth Annual Institute on Privacy and Data Security,* New York: PLI (2009) p 662

the privacy rights of corporate whistleblowers and potential wrongdoers are filed.

13.2 Data Processing

Obviously, companies must be concerned about personal data, but it is the processing of data that normally gets a company in trouble. What is processing? How is it defined? What does it involve?

The European Union considers processing of data as any operation or set of operations performed upon personal data. From a legal perspective, almost any data-related operation involves processing. If you are in the United States, and you are reviewing personal data from an employee situated in the European Union, or your servers in the European Union transfers such information to your server in the United States, you may have violated EU data privacy laws. As Canada's privacy laws are also based on the EU's laws and regulations you also should be concerned if your servers in Canada share personal data with your servers in the U.S. Be careful!

13.3 Other Data

Besides personal data, a company must also consider the risks of unauthorized access or dissemination of other kinds of data. Such data could include various kinds, such as:

- Financial data
- Medical data
- R&D data
- Marketing strategy data
- Technology-related data

Therefore, a company or organization must consider regulatory requirements, global data protection laws, US state laws, and its own compliance policies and corporate regulations when considering how to handle and protect data, as well as the risks surrounding unauthorized access or use of such data. Not only is a company's violation of data privacy laws looked upon seriously, but data theft or lack of appropriate data security systems likewise are frowned upon by society in general but looked upon as inexcusable by an organization's stakeholders. Failure to properly handle and protect data can lead to headaches for everyone concerned.

13.4 Data Processes and Related Risks

When an organization confronts the risk inherent in unauthorized use of its data, it must keep in mind three basic risks involved with data processes before implementing risk management solutions.

- Financial risk: Fines and penalties resulting from privacy laws, EU directive, litigation, litigation costs, U.S. data protection laws, and U.S. state data protection laws
- Intellectual property risks: Loss of competitiveness in the marketplace due to loss of trade secrets or other forms of IP to competitors wherever situated
- Brand risks: Loss of reputation, customer loss, negative publicity, negative reaction of stakeholders, and increased scrutiny of regulators

The above-mentioned risks can be catastrophic when dealing with data and data processes. An organization must confront the three major risks in light of regular corporate data processes, primarily:

- Data usage: Data processes involved with data usage, such as data accessed by specific users
- Data storage: Data stored in servers
- Data transfer: Data transferred to third parties from specific points in a computer network

Each data process or stage of data usage poses specific risks that can harm an organization. In determining the risks a company faces prior to developing an LRM solution, an organization must answer a series of questions such as:

- What data does the organization have and where is it located?
- What kind of data does the company have and how sensitive or confidential is it?
- What processes, if any, are currently in place to protect the data?
- What company policies, if any, currently exist that control data and access to the data?
- What company process or procedures exist, if any, that control access of sensitive data by third parties?
- What company policies or procedures exist, if any, when dealing with personal data, especially personal data from EU countries or jurisdictions with rigorous data privacy laws?

Based on the answers to the questions above, a company can implement LRM solutions that can address and minimize the major risks a company faces when dealing with data, whether personal, financial, or IP related.

13.5 LRM Solutions to the Data Problem

After an organization conducts a risk assessment on data and data usage, it is in a better situation to appreciate the risks it faces regarding its data and can then take steps to implement an LRM solution.

When it comes to the unauthorized access or dissemination of data, a company should consider a solution based upon three key areas using a set of tools to implement the strategy:

- Technology: A policy-based approach using technology to discover and monitor potential data leaks or unauthorized data transmission over networks or mobile devices, such as PDAs, systems, and data repositories.

- Training: A company must develop a process covering unauthorized data transmission to third parties or nonessential personnel. Such processes must be reinforced and implemented by appropriate training programs.
- Management: Management must implement and oversee operational requirements that implement the solutions needed to prevent data leakage.

Regarding data privacy laws, most companies that must deal with the EU directive or similar data privacy regulations can minimize data privacy risks through a combination of the following processes:

- Contractually: use of binding standard contractual clauses that deal with privacy data.
- Binding corporate rules (BCR): codes of conduct accepted by the EU that bind the company to a specific code of practice when dealing personal data. The BCR requires a company to implement adequate safeguards required by the EU.
- Safe Harbor: a voluntary self-certification program available to US companies under certain circumstances.

However, to qualify, companies must adhere to the safe harbor rules, called the Safe Harbor Principles. To qualify, companies must:

- Bring the company's data protection rules into compliance with the Safe Harbor Principles.
- Verify the company is in compliance with the Safe Harbor Principles.
- Complete the certification process.

14

Contract Management

Form: Contract Management Process

14.1 Contract Risk Management

A major area of legal risk for any company is the negotiation, execution, and performance of contracts. Many companies have spent much money creating and/or improving the contract management process. Some companies simply rely on outside counsel to handle its contracts, blissfully unaware that the lack of internal contract risk management controls exposes it in the long run to major legal and business liability—a lawsuit waiting to happen!

A company needs to address many contractual areas prior to drafting contracts as well as managing them. Not only must a company negotiate agreements but it must also manage and comply with the agreements once they have been negotiated and executed. Companies cannot rely on outside legal counsel to do this for them.

Some of the areas that need to be addressed include:

- IP
- Warranties

- Indemnities
- Tax
- Sales and marketing issues
- Responsibilities and obligations
- Deliverables
- Payment obligations
- Industry terms and conditions
- Insurance

Obviously, if a proper contract management system is not in place, some or all the issues above may be affected, causing great harm to the company. Pricing could be impacted, or missed contractual obligations could result in the company's indemnity obligations to cover more than expected. Contractual defenses as well may not be implemented due to the lack of appropriate contracts or contractual terms.

14.1.1 Contract Management Issues

In order for a company's contracts to be negotiated, performed, and executed properly, a number of organizations within a company must work together and coordinate efforts. Depending on the kind of contract, its size, and scope, not only should divisions or business units work together, but appropriate policies and processes must be implemented and followed.

For instance, decision makers within a company need to make informed and timely business decisions prior to execution of a contract, but can only do so based on input from internal stakeholders or division heads. A process needs to be in place to ensure timely advice is provided. Depending on the nature of the risks and issues involved (i.e., billing, tax, etc.) appropriate departments will need to be involved.

A proper LRM audit needs to be conducted to ensure the proper contract management process is in place. Such an audit should cover roles and responsibilities of departments within an organization, the kinds of contracts used by the business units, the major legal and business term that must be addressed, the process for informing the relevant decision makers as to the risks faced, and the process for ensuring the contracts are not only signed but also performed. A contract management process can be very detailed, which is why some companies have failed to adopt the process. Of course, when a company fails to implement a contract management process, it opens itself up to potential legal and financial exposure.

A company's contract management process must allow for negotiation and resolution of major business and legal issues while its customers or vendors are satisfied with the process. Therefore, a company's contract management process must not only allow for proper negotiation and resolution of contractual issues, but must also ensure the company is not exposed to undue risk. Though a company may be willing to assume a moderate level of risk, it may not be willing to accept a greater degree of risk without pricing the risk or cost of risk into its pricing calculations. From an accounting standpoint, a company may wish to increase its reserves as well.

14.1.2 Roles and Responsibilities

A company's various business units as well as Legal, Sales, Risk, Finance, Human Resources, Contract Management (if it exists), and other impacted corporate departments or groups must work together to minimize undue risk to the company and ensure how the risk should be managed.

Roles and responsibilities of certain organizations within a company or corporation normally include:

- Corporate Risk Management: The division head or department head responsible for identifying risk and facilitating mitigation by working with Legal, Business Units, and decision makers. Corporate risk management implements policies and procedures to ensure risk mitigation strategies are pursued throughout the life of the contract.

- Legal: The department responsible for identifying legal risks and available legal options and preparation and maintenance of contracts and contract templates. Also responsible for negotiating legal terms.
- Contract Management: The department responsible for identifying and documenting legal and business issues raised during negotiation of contract terms (if not done by Legal) and escalation of legal and business terms to the correct decision makers within the company. Usually has to notify Legal of complex legal issues.
- Finance: The department responsible for issues including cash flow, time value of money, and reserve calculations.
- Sales: The division or department responsible for communicating with and maintenance of the customer relationship while helping to mitigate risk to the company. Needs to understand basic risk issues.
- Business Units: The division or various departments responsible for identifying the strategic value of the contract. May want contract managers to stay in their unit.
- Human Resources: The department responsible for issues involving personnel management, secondment if needed, noncompetition issues, and other matters having a direct effect on employees.

Other decision makers or internal stakeholders may also be involved besides the groups listed above. The board of directors (BOD), executive committee, CEO, CFO, or controller, etc., may get involved to discuss risk mitigation strategies as is necessary.

14.2 Contract Management Processes

The contract management process, to be effective, must include processes and procedures that identify and resolve certain legal and business issues.

Among those processes and procedure are:

14.2.1 *The Escalations Process*

This is the process in which certain important legal and business risks get escalated to the proper organization for resolution. Such a process should include:

- Identification of the issues
- Communication to relevant stakeholders
- Business impact analysis
- Resolution of issue
- Communication of resolution and documentation of the resolution

14.2.2 *Contract Approvers and Processes*

A process has to be implemented to ensure that:

- All Contract Management/Legal comments have been incorporated into the contract or at least properly considered.
- The contract is ready for execution or for the signature of the other party.
- The most current version of the contract is ready to be uploaded into the database.
- The correct contact names and billing addresses are in the final version of the contract.
- All payment terms are final and correct.

14.2.3 *Standard Billing and Payment Terms*

A company normally has certain standard billing and payment terms in its contracts. Such terms need to be included in the proper agreements. Depending on the kind of contract in question, such terms could include various payment models such as:

- Fixed fee payment
- Time and materials

- Milestone payments
- Maintenance payments
- Payment based on credit

The process should ensure, absent escalation, that the standard billing and payment terms are in the contract as required.

14.2.4 Ownership of Intellectual Property (IP)

One of the most important assets of any company is of course its IP. It, therefore, stands to reason that IP concerns and considerations must be properly reflected in the contract management process. IP concerns include:

- Ownership of IP rights
  - Does the company retain or receive IP rights?
  - Does the other contracting party receive right and title to the IP?
- Retention of IP rights
  - When does the company retain all right, title, and interest in any and all IP?
  - When does the other contracting party retain all right, title, and interest in any and all of the IP?
- Ownership of newly created IP
  - What happens when the company or contracting party creates IP during performance of the contract? This could be in the form of manuals, software, training materials, and other media and information
- Similar works
  - What happens when the company performs similar services for third-party customers?

14.2.5 Typical Customer or Vendor Requests

A company's customers or vendors may typically ask for certain terms in a contract. Such terms could impose undue risk on the company or negatively affect its contractual relations with third parties. The contract management process must address and resolve the issues caused by such requests. Terms typically asked for may include:

- Customer retention of IP rights
- Noncompetition provisions
- Customer ownership of deliverables
- Nonstandard payment terms
- Staffing changes
- Broad indemnity provisions
- Limitation of liability

A company's contracts would or should normally address all of the above-mentioned issues. The contract management process must ensure that the issues are escalated to and resolved by the appropriate stakeholders and that all appropriate terms have been negotiated and addressed in a timely manner.

14.2.6 Preliminary Agreements

A well-thought-out contract management process will contain certain company guidelines and preliminary agreement templates to facilitate the deal. A LRM audit should review any and all preliminary guidelines and document templates to ensure the needs of the company are being met and potential legal and business risks are mitigated. Preliminary agreements include:

- Letter of intent (LOI): Normally a document reflecting the understanding between the company and customer or vendor without creating a binding contractual obligation.

  A corporation's LOI usage guidelines should address subject matter of the LOI, the fact that the parties do not wish to be bound, when a nondisclosure agreement is needed, and under what terms the parties expect to be bound at a later date.

- Memorandum of understanding (MOU): Normally a document for establishing an agreement of critical or major terms between the parties before a full and final contract is negotiated and executed. May have binding terms and conditions.

  A corporation's MOU usage guidelines should address what obligations the company is willing to commit to before negotiating a complete contract, as well as a definition of the framework for negotiation of such as the price, milestones, deliverables, etc.

- Letter of authorization (LOA): Normally a document containing a minimum set of key terms and conditions that the parties must agree upon in order to begin work during contract negotiations. Not always used.

  A corporation's LOA usage guidelines should deal with issues such as IP, liability, price, etc., that may be hard to negotiate after the work has started.

Note: A process must be in place requiring the signature and/ or sign-off of the appropriate corporate officer or officers prior to execution of any of the preliminary agreements. It is best to get the appropriate sign off in writing.

14.3 Miscellaneous Issues

A contract management process must take into account other issues besides the basic contract issues of escalation, contract templates, indemnity clauses, sign-off authority, etc. Several of them are set forth below.

- Sales and marketing practices
- In order for the proper management of contracts, Sales must determine how annual sales, revenue, and profit will be achieved across the various business units. This should be reflected either in a sales and marketing plan or manual involving the account manager, product specialist (if any), credit manager, marketing manager, and business unit manager.
- Business processes
  As the company's IP and other assets are very important, the contract management process should include business processes that protect the company's assets or mitigate risk. Such business processes should include:
- Computer safeguards
- IP safeguards
- Data privacy controls and safeguards
- Information controls and safeguards
- Competition-antitrust
- One of the most important legal and regulatory areas affecting a company and its business practices involves competition, or antitrust. The world's major economic regimes are enthusiastically enforcing antitrust/competition laws and regulations requiring competition guidelines to be not only enforced by a compliance program but implemented in a contract management process. The contract management process should address antitrust issues and enforce antitrust/competition guidelines by implementing processes and procedures that address major antitrust issues such as:
  - Exclusive dealing agreements
  - Discrimination among vendors or customers
  - Benchmarking with competitors on business practices and costs
  - Tying agreements

The contract management process contains many potential legal and business risks if not performed correctly. An LRM program should cover an audit of the contract management process and ensure that it reduces, mitigates, or prevents legal and business risk. It requires the active participation of all major organizations within a company, including Legal, Finance, Sales, HR, and Risk Management. If a company does not have contract management systems in place it needs to either design them or use off-the-shelf contract management software to implement the processes. A number of good off-the-shelf programs are available. However, it is advised that if a company uses an off-the –shelf program that it customize the program to ensure the company's processes and unique concerns are adequately addressed by the software.

15

Foss

Free and open source software (FOSS) issues have increasingly become a major issue for software, telecommunication, and other high-tech companies using FOSS-related software. FOSS-related issues include copyrights and licensing, trademarks, and patents issues that, if not addressed properly, can lead to legal exposure. More and more companies are finding that FOSS is very important. In most situations a FOSS audit is needed to determine what FOSS-related processes are needed.

15.1 What Is FOSS?

When software source code is written, the owner or creator of the source code must decide whether to license it and under what terms. Free open source software implies the source code may be copied and/or modified or distributed free of charge under certain conditions. The problems arise when those using, modifying, and/or distributing FOSS-related software do so without following or applying the terms and conditions of the owner's license. If the copyright owner of particular FOSS software imposes certain conditions on the use and distribution of free and open source code, the conditions must be followed.

15.2 Licenses

The copyright owner can use numerous FOSS licenses. Among them, the most popular is the general public license (GNU), as well as the lesser used lesser general public license (LGPL), which is a variant of the GPL.

Prior to using a GPL or GNU, a company needs to determine what goals it has in using the free open source software, or, if it is writing code, what project specifications are driving the project.

Some owners of FOSS-related software place very few restrictions, if any, on the use of software. Often, the licenses associated with this software are commonly referred to as "BSD" or "BSD-style" licenses. These licenses are known for the bare minimum restrictions that are placed on development and distribution.[1]

15.3 FOSS Violations

Companies or users of FOSS or related software many times face legal liability for violation of FOSS licenses. This problem happens when companies seek to distribute copyleft FOSS code in their own proprietary software, which is closed, non free software. The problem gets worse when companies use FOSS code from subcontractors or vendors that have also failed to properly use FOSS code.

As violation of open source licenses puts companies in jeopardy of being sued for copyright infringement, serious financial, reputational, and legal damages potentially threaten a company. Companies, therefore, have to consider implementation of a FOSS compliance program to minimize risk of exposure to such violations

---

[1] Phillip Koltan, "Keys to Managing a FOSS Compliance Program," The Linux Foundation, http://www. Linuxfoundation.org.

15.4 FOSS Compliance

In 2008, the Court of Appeals for the Federal Circuit in the United States ruled for the first time that open source licenses are enforceable, and those who fail to comply with the conditions of the open source licenses are subject to copyright infringement claims.[2] This ruling has resulted in legal risks for companies using FOSS, especially when a company does not have adequate procedures and policies in place to comply with the open source software licenses.

Therefore, it is vital that companies using open source software on a regular basis establish an LRM process to implement a compliance program covering the use of free open source software. Failure to do so will result in copyright infringement litigation and potential reputational harm.

A growing body of literature covers FOSS compliance. The Linux Foundation has published a white paper on FOSS compliance that covers various aspects of FOSS compliance, including corporate practices needed to establish a FOSS compliance program.[3] Considering the potential legal exposure companies face in using open source software, a FOSS audit and compliance program are excellent LRM tools to minimize legal risk.

---

[2] Jacobson v. Katzer, 535F3d1373 (Fed. Cir. 2008).

[3] Phillip Koltan, Supra 1.

16

Outsourcing

Form: Outsourcing Agreement

Outsourcing is another tool that can be used to mitigate, transfer, or reduce risk. Usually, outsourcing involves an arrangement under which a company transfers responsibility for the performance of an internal business function to an outside service provider.

A company may mitigate or transfer risk by turning over high-risk operations to a third party that is skilled in handling such operations. I was involved once in outsourcing a data center of a client to a third party that was skilled in maintaining such data centers as the client had problems in managing.

Outsourcing certain operations may not only save the company money and reduce financial risk, but may also reduce the risk of employee-related claims as well as risks associated with that function. Outsourcing, if used properly, can be quite effective in reducing and mitigating risk.

16.1 Structure

Outsourcing a departments function or even division normally involves:

- Providing a third party with hardware and equipment
- Developing and managing software or often deliverables
- Transfer of some key employees

Companies seek to minimize and transfer legal risk; outsourcing is a great tool if used properly. Normally companies will not outsource core functions of the company that generate cash but can outsource noncore functions involving such departments as:

- IT
- HR
- Facilities (mail, call center, food, maintenance)
- Training
- Legal

16.2 Outsourcing Arrangements

Outsourcing of a function involves the use and implementation of an outsourcing agreement that covers not only the transfer of the particular business function but the provision of services by the outsourcing company (i.e., service provider). Prior to developing the agreement, however, the company must really sit down and decide whether the outsourcing of a business function is worth it. What is the true basis of the decision to outsource and will it minimize or transfer risk? To answer that question, companies often conduct a study or approach potential outsourcing vendors to see what data they have to justify the decision to outsource.

There are numerous outsourcing arrangements companies can use to transfer risk, including:

- IT
  - Help desk
  - Software maintenance
  - Network management
  - Data center
- Corporate process
  - Claims processing
  - Payroll and employee benefits
  - Credit card processing
- Management
  - Labor based services such as:
    - HR
    - Mail room
    - Legal
    - Compliance

16.3 Issues and Concerns

Before plunging ahead and outsourcing certain noncore functions, a business needs to be aware of the legal risks it may face. Among the risks are:

- Labor and employment laws of the jurisdiction in which the outsourcing takes place
  - Is the vendor an established entity?
  - Is the vendor deemed an independent contractor under applicable laws?
  - Will it involve former employees who transfer over?
  - How much control will the company retain over workers?
- Restrictions in contracts
  - Are there contractual severance provisions in contracts of employees who are outsourced?
  - Bonus plan issues.
  - ERISA benefit plan issues.

The contract

An outsourcing arrangement by its very nature entails long-term relationship and the delivery of an ongoing service. Therefore, the contract is vital to the success of the outsourcing arrangement, especially the portion covering performance of services, which is normally set forth in a statement of work, or "SOW". The SOW is arguably the most important part of the agreement.

Typically, the SOW sets forth and defines:

- The scope of services of each party
- Pricing
- The duties, functions, and responsibilities of the parties involved
- The applicable specifications, quantities, types, etc., as they relate to the services to be performed

It is of vital importance, therefore, that if you use an outsourcing arrangement you clearly define the specifications, scope, and responsibilities of both parties in the SOW. Some examples of SOW specifications include:

- Transfer of equipment leases
- Types of hardware to be deployed
- Quantities of storage
- Deliverables to be provided
- Software licenses to be transferred
- Program modules to be migrated over
- Personnel to be transferred
- Project phases of arrangement

To help transfer or mitigate the risk involved in outsourcing itself, the following provisions or "tools" should be used in the contract and SOW:

- Performance levels

- Limitation of liability
- Insurance
- Changes in business
- Limited warranty
- Choice of law or dispute resolution mechanism
- Data security provisions

16.4 Dispute Resolution

Though dispute resolution processes are addressed in a different chapters of this book, as an outsourcing contract is a major contract, it is wise to mention it here as well.

Because outsourcing is a unique arrangement, it is best to consider what aspects of a company's organizational efforts should be used in facilitating and maintaining the outsourcing relationship. I think it best to consider management of the outsourcing relationship to be of primary importance when resolving disputes. When considering dispute management, a company should structure such process in the contract and SOW as follows:

- Corporate management services
- Dedicated teams to manage outsourcing relationship
- Escalation of dispute to management and then executive management
- Nonbinding mediation
- Binding arbitration

SUMMARY

The implementation of an LRM program requires a risk assessment or a risk audit. Only through a risk assessment can a company identify the major areas of legal risk as well as evaluate the strengths and weaknesses in its current risk processes. Such risk assessment should only be conducted after the company has established goals and objectives in which to evaluate the results of the audit.

Normally an LRM audit would be conducted in phases. In the basic approach, which can be used as a model for the LRM audit, phases include: phase 1, in which the company decides to do a risk review; phase 2, in which the risk identification takes place; phase 3, in which tools are used to identify the severity of the risk; phase 4, in which a critical risk analysis is conducted to determine probability of impact; and phase 5, in which the action plan is implemented.

Numerous processes can be implemented to mitigate legal risk. For manufacturing companies, product liability remains a series of legal exposures. Besides basic product liability defenses, companies also have to concern themselves with design risk management processes as well. Besides design risk management processes and product liability mitigation processes, companies should also consider outsourcing of certain functions as another form of LRM, or risk management.

Many risks are inherent in a company's use of data. Risks exist everywhere, from unauthorized access of data via hacking, a stolen laptop, third-party vendors, inadequate security systems, increased regulatory oversight, and unenforced privacy policies. In today's technology-oriented society, data leakage and data privacy risks pose enormous threats to a company's financial and reputational well-being and must be taken seriously.

PART 3

Legal Risk Management Strategies: Pre-litigation

The goal of legal risk management, or LRM, is to minimize, transfer, or reduce exposure to legal risk. Obviously, to have a successful LRM program, a company must think proactively—prior to the filing of litigation or prior to the commencement of government investigations or levying of fines and penalties. What LRM strategies can be used prior to litigation that can reduce risk? What programs and processes, if properly executed, will minimize or mitigate the threat of litigation or government investigations? Many processes can reduce or minimize legal and financial exposure, but the most important are set forth in this section.

17

Employee Benefit Plans

17.1 Employee Benefit Plans Audit

One of the most important audits a risk manager/in-house counsel should conduct as part of a LRM program is an audit of employee benefit plans. Many countries offer employee benefit plans, pensions, or related schemes in accordance with local laws.

In the U.S., employee benefit plans or retirement benefit plans are subject to the requirements of the employee Retirement Income Security Act of 1974, as amended (ERISA)[1]. It is very important, for reasons set forth in this chapter that a LRM program cover an ERISA audit as well as a compliance review. Failure to do so, could subject a company in the U.S. as well as the company's board of directors to $$$ in fines and penalties, not only from the Department of Labor's standpoint but from the I.R.S. standpoint as well.

---

[1] ERISA is codified at 29 U.S.C. Sec 15. However, parts of ERISA laws covering tax issues are also found in the U.S. IRS code.

17.2 Employee Benefit Plans Review

Regulations adopted pursuant to ERISA set forth requirements respecting employee retirement and welfare benefit plans (the "Plan"), include:

- Reporting and disclosure requirements
- Fiduciary responsibility
- Administration and enforcement
- Participation and vesting

ERISA requires that health and welfare plans be set forth in a written document which describes the benefit and the operation of the Plan. The document must identify who is responsible for the control, management and operation of the Plan. The Plan must also have recordkeeping systems to track the flow of funds and written. Materials to provide to Plan participants.

The general review of a compliance audit should focus on three areas:

- Fiduciary responsibility
- Plan documents
- Process, procedure, reporting and disclosure requirements

17.3 Fiduciary Considerations

ERISA sets standards of conduct for employee benefit plan sponsors and others who exercise discretion in managing a plan or plan assets. Therefore, use of discretion in administering and managing an employee benefit plan or controlling the plan's assets makes that person a fiduciary to the extent of such control or discretion. Fiduciary status is determined based upon the functions performed.

Each Plan must have a named fiduciary; however, a person does not need to be named to be a fiduciary; who jointly or severally controls and manages the operation and administration of the Plan. The Plan instrument may actually designate the named fiduciary or may specify a procedure for naming the fiduciary by the employer.

ERISA sets forth the standards and rules of conduct for plan fiduciaries. Plan fiduciaries are required under ERISA to fulfill a number of duties including:

- A fiduciary must act solely in the interest of plan participants and their beneficiaries and with the exclusive purpose of providing benefits to them.
- A fiduciary must carry out their duties prudently
- A fiduciary must follow plan documents
- A fiduciary must diversify investments
- A fiduciary must pay only reasonable plan expenses

One measure of prudence is the process used to carry out the fiduciary responsibility. Acting under established written procedures which identify Plan fiduciaries and the specific scope of each fiduciary's duty provides a fundamental framework around which to develop programs designed to minimize potential fiduciary liability. Fiduciary liability therefore typically arises from the process, not the actual decision.

Normally, a company is the Plan Sponsor and named fiduciary for the employee benefit and retirement plan including a 401(k) Plan. The company will have fiduciary responsibilities for the employee welfare benefit plans. As the company acts through its' board, the board may be liable.

A fiduciary who breaches any responsibility or duty under ERISA may be personally liable to make good any losses to the Plan resulting from the breach. All fiduciaries have potential liability for the actions of their co-fiduciaries. Breaches of fiduciary responsibility can give rise to civil and criminal penalties, which can be enormous. This has been opened by the U.S Supreme Court. The U.S. Supreme Court has held that individual employee may bring an action for "appropriate equitable relief" under ERISA against an employer for breaching its fiduciary duties (Vanity Corp. V. Howe).[2]

17.4 Settlor Considerations

Not all functions relating to the operation of employee benefit plan are fiduciary functions. The law recognizes "settlor" functions where the Plan Sponsor is acting in its employer capacity. "Settlor" functions include business decisions respecting employee benefit plans.

• Establishment of an employee benefit plan
• Determination of the benefit package
• Features to include in the plan
• Plan termination
• Plan design changes

It is important to recognize where the company's board is acting in a fiduciary capacity or on behalf of the employer in a non-fiduciary capacity. It is critical to document process the board uses to carry out their fiduciary function and that Plan procedures are followed in carrying out Plan Sponsor functions.

17.5 Plan Documents, Process, Procedures and Reporting

Deficiencies in documents, processes and procedures can lead to legal exposure and/or liability for:

• Fiduciary matters
• Tax liabilities
• Civil penalties
• Reporting and disclosure requirements apply to both Employee Retirement Benefit Plans and Employee Welfare Benefit Plans.

---

[2] Vanity Corp. V. Howe, 116 S. Ct 1065 (1996)

A company has reporting and disclosure obligations to the:

- Government
- Participants

In the U.S., an organization's 401(K) Plan is normally a "Qualified" defined contribution retirement benefit plan. "Qualified" Plans can provide significant tax advantages if Internal Revenue Code requirements are met. The Internal Revenue Code requirements relate to "form" and "operation" of the Plan. The Internal Revenue Code imposes excise taxes intended as penalties on a wide variety of prohibited transactions between a Qualified Plan and an employer, trustee, or other disqualified person, subject to a number of statutory exemptions.

17.6 Compliance Audit

A compliance review should be conducted to determine what a general pattern and practice has been implemented respecting actions taken by the company with respect to both the retirement and health & welfare benefit plans usually the Human Resources Department may be involved with ERISA obligations. How has it conducted the 401(k) or Employee Benefit and Retirement Program?

As a prudent fiduciary, the process used by the company select and monitor the specialists it retains to carry out functions respecting the plans is the focus for determining whether the Board of Directors acted in a prudent fashion in selecting and retaining the advisors. A LRM Compliance audit should cover the following:

- Secure information and documents submitted to the company connection with the retention of service providers
- Obtain copies of engagement letters and service agreements
- Review compensation agreements
- Review reports supplied by or relating to the performance of each service provider

- Ensure that the agreement with the service providers sets forth the specific responsibilities of the company and the service provider under the agreement
- Consider indemnification and insurance requirements
- Document periodic reviews of service providers performance
- Review current insurance programs respecting fiduciary coverage
- Review By Laws respecting indemnification

17.7 Recommended Actions

Board considerations should encompass many areas, including:

- Establishment of a committee of the Board to oversee employee benefit plan matters
- Review of the fiduciary responsibilities and plan administration activities respecting retirement and health & welfare benefit plans
- Consider delegation of authority and responsibility for certain activities respecting the management and operation of the plans
- Establish written procedures which identify fiduciaries to whom responsibility is delegated and the specific scope of each fiduciaries responsibility

17.8 Compliance Considerations

A general employee retirement and welfare benefit plan compliance review is highly recommended in many organizations. Not only in the U.S. but elsewhere as many countries have laws and regulations concerning benefit plans. However, in the U.S., companies face great exposure if they fail to implement proper procedures and safeguards in respect to ERISA requirements. Therefore, I cannot stress enough the importance of a legal audit of employee retirement and welfare programs or benefit plan programs considering the immense legal exposure a company and /or its BOD may face.

18

Compliance

Form: Compliance Policy
Form: Compliance Manual

18.1 What Is Compliance?

Many countries now require companies to implement compliance policies for legal reasons. Some companies have implemented compliance policies for brand image and other reasons as well. A compliance program, properly implemented, not only increases a company's brand image but reinforces ethical behavior, which in turn minimizes violation of local laws by upholding compliance of financial and legal rules.

To understand compliance, one needs to review the history of compliance in the United States.

US Compliance History

18.1.1 Background

- In November 1991, an innovative piece of legislation was enacted in the United States that had an important and profound impact on corporate America. This legislation in turn has reverberated around the world.

- The legislation was the US Federal Sentencing Guidelines ("Guidelines").

18.1.2 The Guidelines

- The Guidelines are used by judges to determine the appropriate sentence for corporations convicted of a federal crime.
- According to the Guidelines, a corporation may be sentenced or fined for federal offenses connected with antitrust, securities, bribery, fraud, money laundering, criminal business activities, extortion, embezzlement, conspiracy, etc. As you can see it is quite broad and covers many "illegal" activities.

When deciding on an appropriate sentence, judges were for the first time asked to consider whether the corporation had an "effective compliance program" before the violation took place or, in other words, whether the corporation took appropriate steps to prevent and detect violations of law. Therefore, in order for courts to reduce or mitigate criminal sanctions, companies must now have a compliance program in place. The Guidelines were amended in 2004 (Revised Guidelines).[1]

18.1.3 The Revised Guidelines

- The Revised Guidelines recognize that effective compliance and ethics requires more than policies and procedures, it also entails a focus on organizational culture that promotes law abidance. In other words, a major focus is on compliance and ethics.

---

[1] Federal Sentencing Guidelines for Organizations (revised and amended as of Nov. 1, 2004).

- For the first time, a set of laws creates a legal mandate for compliance. It looks at:
  - Incentives
  - Requirements
  - Guidance
  - A focus on ethical behavior

18.1.4 *The Revised Guidelines*

- The Revised Guidelines recognize seven elements in a proper compliance program.
- The current Revised Guidelines list seven elements of an "effective compliance program" as being:
  - Compliance standards and procedures (a code of conduct should exist)
  - Oversight by high-level personnel (the Board must oversee the program)
  - Due care when delegating authority (due care in hiring employees)
  - Effective communication of standards and procedure (training)
  - Auditing/monitoring/reporting systems must be in place
  - Compliance must be promoted and enforced consistently throughout the organization
  - There must be an appropriate response from the company after a violation has been detected

18.1.5 *Failure to Enact Compliance*

- In February 1996, in what was the largest criminal fine in US history, a New York federal court, following the Guidelines, sentenced Daiwa Bank (Japan) to pay a $340 million fine.[2]

---

[2] See United States v The Daiwa Bank, S.D.N.Y. 95 Cr. (KMW)

- The case involved a bank employee who lost $1.1 billion in unauthorized trades.
- Prosecution arose out of a report of an unauthorized, off-the-books trading scheme—bank officials conspired to conceal the losses from bank regulators for more than two months.
- The two main reasons for the fine:
  - "Lack of a meaningful compliance program"
  - "Consequent failure to report the employee's wrongdoing"

18.1.6 Lessons

Foreign companies doing business in the United States can learn an especially important lesson from Daiwa Bank. Primarily, foreign companies doing business in the United States must realize they have to comply with U.S. laws and regulations. Daiwa Bank could have avoided the criminal fine had it followed the requirements of the U.S. Sentencing Guidelines.

18.1.7 The United States

In implementing a compliance program in conformity with U.S. law and in compliance with specific laws, a company shows it fully appropriates U.S. laws and regulations. By developing such a compliance program, a company understands in general terms the requirements of U.S. law.

18.2 Establishment of Compliance Program

The establishment of a compliance program anywhere in the world usually consists of adopting a company code of conduct, with perhaps specific policies governing local conditions. However, because of the U.S. requirements, many organizations have adapted compliance policies that conform to U.S. standards. Because of the Revised Guidelines, specific elements to a valid compliance program are required. They are:

18.2.1 US Compliance Program

- The basics—what is needed?
  - A code of conduct
  - Local codes of business ethics (and other company policies) covering each country in which a company does business
  - Local training on all aspects, such as antitrust, employee issues, etc.
  - A system to report suspected wrongdoing to the company
  - An anonymous reporting system allowing employees to report wrongdoing anonymously

18.2.2 Code of Conduct

A company's compliance programs' code of conduct should incorporate various principles. Primarily, five basic principles should be followed or reflected in the code. The five principles a company's compliance code of conduct should incorporate are as follows:

- The company complies with local laws and ethical standards of society.
- The company maintains and promotes an ethical organizational corporate culture.
- The company respects customers, shareholders, and employees.
- The company cares for the environment as well as the health, and safety of its customers and society.
- The company is a socially responsible corporate citizen.

18.2.3 U.S. Compliance Program Code of Conduct

To establish an "effective compliance program" under the guidelines and other U.S. laws, a foreign company normally goes beyond its local code or domestic code of conduct. Its employees must be familiar with the specific laws that govern their conduct in the jurisdiction in which they work.

If a company has a branch or division in the United States, it must have a U.S. Code of Ethics, which is designed to inform employees in the United States about the specific laws and standards governing their conduct. Having a compliance program is mandated by the U.S. Sentencing Guidelines.

18.2.4 *The U.S. Compliance Program Local Codes of Business Ethics (and Other Policies)*

- A U.S. Compliance and Code of Ethics (and other policies) should cover at a minimum approximately twenty-two different areas. An employee handbook should perhaps cover another forty or more.
- U.S. Code of Conduct
- Principle 1. The company complies with laws and ethical standards:
  - Nondiscrimination, anti-harassment, and anti-retaliation
  - Drugs and alcohol
  - Wage and hour laws
  - Americans with Disabilities Act
  - Employment at will
  - Political contributions and activities
  - Personal political contributions
  - Antitrust law and competitive practices
  - Foreign Corrupt Practices Act
  - Government contracts (if it does government work)
  - Government relations-dealing with government regulators
  - Government reports
- Principle 2. The company maintains an ethical organizational culture:
  - Company property, confidential information
  - Intellectual property and property of others
  - Accurate books and records

- Computer hardware and software, e-mail
- Confidentiality of client information
- Accounting policies
- Conflicts of interest
- Nondiscrimination, anti-harassment, and anti-retaliation
- Drugs and alcohol
- Principle 3. The company respects customers, shareholders, and employees.
  - Procurement
- Principle 4. The company cares for the environment, health, and safety of its employees and the public.
  - Environments, safety, and health
- Principle 5. The company is a responsible corporate citizen.
  - Compliance procedures

18.2.5 Compliance Training

To have an effective compliance program, a company must also hold compliance training after it "launches" the program. Areas of training should be covered and how the training should be given is of major interest.

It is best if the company offers local compliance training covering the relevant laws and practices where people are located. Training can be given in person, online via web-based training, or by other media. It must be given on a regular basis.

18.2.6 Local Training

- Training on the code of conduct can be given by HR or by Legal.
- Local training in antitrust, anti-harassment, anti-discrimination, and anti-retaliation, ethics, illegal business practices, financial integrity, customs, etc.
- The majority of the local training will be in person and online.
- The goal is to equip employees to handle compliance issues.

- Training should help employees to identify potential wrongdoing.
- Training should help employees understand their role in the compliance scheme.
- It should let them know what to report and how to report.

18.2.7 The U.S. Compliance Program: Reporting Wrongdoing

- In the United States, having an effective reporting system has come to mean one that encourages reporting by allowing for a variety of reporting avenues including anonymous reporting systems.
- If an employee was limited to one avenue of reporting (i.e., to his supervisor), it is likely he would not report wrongdoing if his supervisor was involved.
- In the United States, a company should allow for employee reporting normally as follows.

18.2.8 Employee Reporting

All employees are required to promptly report all known or suspected violations of applicable laws or of the compliance program, including corporate policies. Reports of such violations shall be promptly made to a manager; the compliance officer, if any; HR; or to the Law Department. If any employee wishes, he or she may report violations anonymously via an anonymous e-mail (or by phone) system. All reports should be promptly and thoroughly investigated.

To the extent possible and permitted by law, the company must take reasonable precautions to maintain the confidentiality of those individuals who report legal or compliance-related violations.

18.3 Training Programs

Training programs may vary depending on the needs of a particular company. Training programs may consist of instructor-led training, Internet-based, or e-learning programs or even a combination of both. It is up to the company to decide which training program fits the needs of its employees as well as suits its budgetary constraints. In fact, companies in the United States are scrambling around trying to decide on how to handle training programs for the BOD and executive management that is required which includes deciding on what form the training should take, its content as well as the frequency of the training.

18.4 Risk Assessment of Compliance Programs

A risk assessment or LRM audit is vital in the implementation and continued success of any compliance program. Not only does the U.S. Federal Sentencing Guidelines require a periodic risk assessment of a compliance program, but conducting a periodic risk assessment has an upside as well. By conducting a periodic or annual assessment of the compliance program, not only is the company or organization receiving valuable feedback on the program from employees and management which will help it improve the compliance program but it is also will be in compliance with the U.S. Federal Sentencing Guidelines.

By conducting an LRM audit of the compliance program, a company should be able to:

- Review and modify existing corporate processes.
- Update current compliance training, if needed.
- Modify the Compliance Department structure if needed.
- Add additional policies and or training programs.
- Add additional manpower to comply with the compliance needs of the corporation if necessary.

18.5 Legal Risk Management Reasons for a Compliance Program

In the past twenty-five years, numerous companies have been racked by scandals resulting from the absence of compliance.

To name a few:

Companies	Impact
Enron	Bankruptcy
Worldcom	Bankruptcy
Parmalat	Bankruptcy
JP Morgan Chase, Citi	>$2 B penalty fine
Adelphia	$715 M penalty fine

Individuals—Criminal	Sentence
Bernie Ebbers—Worldcom CEO	25 years
Dennis Kozlowski—Tyco CEO	8–25 years
Timothy Rigas—Adelphia CEO	20 years
Andrew Fastow—Enron CEO	10 years
Fronklin Brow—RiteAid CEO	10 years

A company that fails to implement a compliance program may suffer the following:

- Indictment of executives and other managers
- Loss of resources
- Loss of market cap
- Loss of reputation
- Negative impact on the corporate brand

But also, it can affect stakeholders such as:

Stakeholders

Shareholders

Creditors

Employees

Customers

Suppliers

Local Communities

Retirees

In order to minimize or avoid many of the legal and financial issues discussed above, a company should:
- Create a basic compliance system
  - For preventing problems
  - For detecting problems
  - For responding and remedying compliance issues
- Create a culture of compliance
  - Foundation of competitiveness
  - Priority
  - Instill values of ethics
- The key to implementation
  - Senior management must commit to compliance. Management cannot keep a blind eye to problems.
  - Proper checks and balances must be created in the business processes.
  - Compliance must be built into all business processes.

In the United States, companies must implement a sound compliance system in order for directors of the company to discharge their fiduciary responsibilities.[3]

A well-drafted and implemented compliance policy can go a long way to reduce legal risk before litigation arises. World-class companies are driving compliance throughout their organizations. They understand that besides complying with legal requirements, rigorous financial and legal compliance leads to ethical actions that not only minimize legal risk but benefit the company's reputation and ultimately the bottom line, thereby protecting the company's brand.

---

[3] Carole Basri and Irving Kagan, *Corporate Legal Departments*, 3rd ed., PLI, 2004, 11–4 citing in re Caremark Int'l Inc. Derivative Litig, 698 A.2d. 959 (Del. Ch, 1996).

19

Record Retention

Form: Records Retention Program

19.1 Information Retention

Information retention, or "records retention," as it is normally called, is one of the largest sources of potential legal risk (and related financial risk) that companies face. What records a company saves, destroys, or erases may in fact determine the company's fate in litigation. Massive governmental fines and penalties have been levied against companies because of records that were improperly kept or that were uncovered in antitrust investigations, antidumping investigations, etc.

A business must consider the risk of keeping documents, especially electronic documents such as e-mail over an extended period of time. Obviously a business wants to protect valuable information as long as it has value. On the other hand, an organization has to be sensitive to the legal risks posed by saving records and documents past legal requirements of a particular situation.

In essence, we have a balancing act. How does a company balance the needs of business with legal requirements? The issue is not really a legal problem per se but a business problem with legal issues. The legal risk, however, of a nonexistent information retention program can be enormous, and, therefore, should be properly addressed in an LRM program.

How does a company handle retention of documents? What legal requirements exist, and how are they implemented? Strict mandatory standards exist in some countries.

In the United States, the law requires an information retention policy (IRP) that

- retains information at least as long as required by law,
- is applied consistently and systematically,
- allows quick retrieval, and
- can be suspended effectively, if required.

What are the risks of noncompliance?
- Huge fines and penalties
  - The act of losing documents that may be considered evidence in litigation or failing to preserve evidence once legal proceedings appear reasonably likely to occur may damage a company financially and/or its reputation. Note what happened to Arthur Andersen and Enron, etc.
- Huge cost of dealing with information in legal proceedings
- Huge expense of keeping too many documents, especially e-mail
- Not properly implemented

Many companies have an IRP, which, unfortunately, is never properly implemented or followed by employees. Thus, the IRP may at least be ineffective or, at worst, not recognized by courts as a legitimate IRP. This opens the door to fines, sanctions, and worse. Make certain if your company has an IRP that it is properly implemented and followed. If your company does not have an IRP—create and implement one now!

19.2 Risk Assessment: A Suggested Action

A company must ensure it has a viable business / legal oriented IRP in place. A risk assessment must be conducted to determine if one exists. Usually, when a company conducts a risk assessment it will find:

- No suspension procedure exists.
- There has been no auditing of documents.
- The retention policy, if it exists, is antiquated and not equated for the current electronic environment.
- E-mail is not handled correctly.
- The IRP has not been properly implemented or communicated.
- Employees not only are unaware of the IRP but are not following it.

19.3 E-mail

E-mail has become a very important concern when implementing an effective information retention policy or IRP. This is primarily due to E-discovery issues resulting from litigation, which will be discussed later in Chapter 21. The main issue involving e-mail is how long e-mail should be maintained on a computer hard drive before it is deleted. E-mail issues may entail the following:

- No proper archiving of e-mail
- Not properly backed up if needed
- Not properly deleted (i.e., if not accidentally lost, it may be kept forever, resulting in huge costs to review and produce)

An example of potential E-discovery costs because of E-mail is as follows:

1. Preservation	
Preservation notices	$5,000
2. Collection	
Collection from data sources	$11,000
3. Staging	
Preprocessing	$2,000
Processing	$11,000
4. Review	
Contract attorney review	$50,000
Hosting	$10,000
5. Production	$15,000
Total	$99,000

In line with the above referenced E-discovery cost allocation, the table set forth above is a typical example of costs directly associated with a review of ESI for discovery:

- This cost example is based upon a typical review of electronic content to provide a frame of reference.
- This example is for a review of content collected from twenty-five custodians with thirty gigabytes of data.
- The costs are mainly for the discovery review and production life cycle and exclude legal and consulting fees.

19.4 Action Plan

Once a company has conducted a risk assessment of its IRP, it should implement an action plan to address any risk posed by inadequacies of the IRP. At a minimum the following steps are recommended:

- Draft a comprehensive IRP that addresses all documents, including electronic documents.
- Clean up any old information. Records that are no longer required to be kept legally should be destroyed or deleted unless valid business reasons exist to keep them.
- Upper management should approve of the new IRP.
- Departmental retention coordinators should be appointed to drive the new IRP in each department.
- The new IRP must be rolled out to all employees. This may entail marketing the IRP to each department.
- There should be periodic reminders via e-mail, brochures, or posters reminding all employees of the IRP.
- There should be quarterly status meetings with all department coordinators.
- Annual audit: there should be an annual compliance audit to check on the IRP, especially e-mail.

20

Management of E-mail

One of the major business and legal risks a company faces is e-mail. E-mail is now the primary source of all office communication. Over 80 percent of all corporate communications is via e-mail. Over 95 percent of all corporate data created is comprised of e-mail. In fact, over 75 percent of an organization's IP resides in e-mails and attachments. E-mail has become so pervasive in a company that more than 40 percent of all data is not connected to a paper format or tangible medium—it just remains ESI.

The risk inherent in e-mail is due to its instantaneous publication. In other words, e-mail is instantaneous, efficient, and quite user-friendly. The problem is not only does it take up a great deal of space on a company's server, but it is wrongly assumed to be private by most employees. This poses great risk to a company. Let's look at the risks of e-mail.

- E-mail can be forwarded to unintended recipients who get on the e-mail chain.
- Many companies have implemented policies that define e-mail residing on company computers as company property and specifically allow access to knowledge or content of the writer or recipient.

- E-mail is "discoverable" in litigation.
- E-mail memorializes tentative/preliminary opinions that cannot always be explained away.
- E-mail, especially in the U.S. provides a ready source for potential "smoking gun" evidence that can be used against the writer and company.
- E-mail establishes a fact/activity trail based on e-mail date/time stamps—plaintiff lawyers can use e-mail to build detailed histories.
- E-mail is hard to delete once sent.
- Computers maintain a FAT ("file allocation table"); deleting e-mail may only remove the file name from the FAT.
- Data in whole or part can reside in various locations on the hard disk until "overwritten."
- Data is overwritten on a random basis.
- Reconstruction of deleted files is possible through forensic analysis.

Therefore, a company must view e-mail as a necessary evil—one that is a good, efficient business tool that brings with it inherent legal risks.

20.1 Management

A company needs to manage the legal risks of e-mail in several ways.

- E-mail must be part of the document or records retention program. A well-drafted records retention program will cover e-mail destruction, e-mail preservation during litigation, and under other circumstances.
- E-mail training

A company must train its employees as to the risks of e-mail. Employees must be trained to assume:

- E-mail will be requested in subpoenas or through discovery or otherwise inadvertently or purpose fully disclosed to third parties.
- E-mail will be obtained by people seeking to use them against the company.
- If e-mail can be misconstrued, it will be misconstrued.
- E-mail policy

A company must create and implement an e-mail policy and associated processes informing employees that it will monitor e-mail and take action against those who send harassing, malicious, or offensive e-mail to others.

20.2 Training

E-mail training should be made part of the compliance training program. Private attorneys as well as governmental entities can use e-mail against companies in lawsuits or investigations, such as:

- Product liability lawsuits
- Sexual harassment lawsuits
- DOJ antitrust investigations
- FCC or CPSC product safety investigations
- Other governmental investigations

The press, external critics, and watchdog groups may also use e-mail against a company as well.

- Training should mandate employees treat e-mail with care.
- Users treat e-mail too casually and should be cautious.
- E-mail should be treated in the same manner as a memo or letter.
- Employees should be encouraged to reread e-mails and think carefully about their contents before they send the e-mail.
- E-mail should only be circulated to those who need to know.

- Company e-mail should only be used for business reasons.
- E-mail should not be used to transmit trade secrets or other form of IP to third parties without executive approval.
- E-mail should not be used to restrict a company's rights or enlarge its obligations.

20.3 E-mail Issues

A company needs to take e-mail management seriously. Though a convenient form of communication, e-mail is hard to delete and can be used by third parties against a company in litigation or by the government in an investigation. It is too easy to use. A LRM program must address e-mail management issues. Such issue can range from litigation issues to data and records management issues as well.

21

E-discovery

Form: E-discovery Policy

21.1 What Is E-discovery?

One of the most important LRM processes a company needs to implement is the E-discovery management process. But why ?

E-discovery is basically the right of any party in litigation (especially in the United States) to demand electronically stored information (ESI). Of course, a party's right to ESI during litigation is subject to the local laws and legal norms of where the lawsuit is brought. In some jurisdictions it is rare; in others it is used often. When it comes to US litigation, however, the lack of adequate e-discovery processes can be fatal. Foreign companies or individuals doing business in the United States (and some U.S. companies too) fail to realize the importance of ESI and E-discovery until it is too late.

21.1.1 E-discovery in the United States

US law recognizes a party's right to seek ESI in discovery. It mandates disclosure of a copy and/or location of ESI and also allows the requesting party to specify form(s) of production of the ESI documents. If the forms are not specified, the default forms are as stored or reasonable format. The burden of providing ESI can be staggering for a variety of reasons such as:

- Cost of locating all ESI
- Time and energy to locate all relevant ESI
- Time and energy to collect and review ESI
- Cost of production of ESI

The problem facing companies when dealing with ESI is that ESI-related technologies have become numerous and complex. The ability to locate, retrieve, collect, review, and produce relevant ESI (including e-mail) may determine a company's future, once it is involved in litigation. The reasons for this include:

- Some reports estimate that approximately 80 percent of costs of litigation are related to discovery, including E-discovery.
- Litigation involving E-discovery in the United States can be costly.
- Failure to have an adequate E-discovery process can be fatal.
- US Federal Rules or Civil Procedure and US case law (*Zubulake v. UBS*, etc.) have created significant issues and costs.[1]

21.2 E-discovery Obligations: US Laws and Case Law

The Federal Rules of Civil Procedure (FRCP) defines a party's ESI obligations in federal litigation.

- E-discovery

- Preservation of evidence

---

[1] Zubulake v. UBS Warburg LLC, 217 F.R.D. 309 (S.D.N.Y, 2003). Note there are five Zubulake cases in total.

- Federal Rules of Civil Procedure (FRCP) early focus on parties' obligation to preserve evidence as early as possible
- Rule changes address e-discovery
  - Early consideration of discovery plan
  - Early consideration of privilege issues
  - Accessibility of electronically stored information (ESI)
  - Formats for production of ESI
  - Federal Rules of Civil Procedure
    - Rule 26
      - Committee note: "a responding party should produce electronically stored information that is relevant, not privileged, and reasonably accessible, subject to the (b)(2)C limitations that apply to all discovery.
      - "The responding party must also identify, by category or type, the sources containing potentially responsive information that it is neither searching nor producing. The identification should, to the extent possible, provide enough detail to enable the requesting party to evaluate the burdens and costs of providing the discovery and the likelihood of finding responsive information on the identified sources . . ."
- Preservation of evidence
  - Litigation hold
  - Zubulake V [*Zubulake v. UBS*, 229, F.R.D. 422 (S.D.N.Y. 2004)]
    - Requires outside counsel to make certain that all potentially relevant information is identified and placed "on hold."
    - "To do this counsel must become fully familiar with her client's document retention architecture. This will invariably involve speaking with information technology personnel who can explain system wide back up procedures and the actual (as opposed to theoretical) implementation of the firm's recycling

policy. It will also involve communicating with the 'key players' in the litigation, in order to understand how they stored information . . ."

- Preservation of evidence
  - "The obligation to preserve evidence arises when the party has notice that the evidence is relevant to litigation or when a party should have known that the evidence may be relevant to future litigation . . ." (*Fujitsu Ltd. v. Federal Express Corp.*, 247 F3d 423, 436 (2d Cir. 2001)

Not only does the "hold" requirement apply to a company's ESI but to backup tapes as well. The court in Zubulake addressed this issue:

- Litigation hold
  - Zubulake V [*Zubulake v. UBS*, 229, F.R.D. 422 (S.D.N.Y. 2004)]
    - "As a general rule, that litigation hold does not apply to inaccessible backup tapes (e.g., those that are maintained solely for the purpose of disaster recovery) . . . which may continue to be recycled on the schedule set forth in the company's policy. On the other hand, if backup tapes are accessible (i.e., actively used for information retrieval), then such tapes would likely be subject to the litigation hold . . ."

21.3 Information Technology (IT)

In order to comply with the E-discovery rules and regulation as well as case law in the United States, a company (including its in-house counsel) must closely look at the IT network in order to locate where all relevant ESI is located. Only after a company thoroughly searches and collects data can it then review and collate it.

21.4 Management of E-discovery Process

There are five basic steps to the E-discovery process that must be or should be managed by in-house counsel (or outside counsel if no in-house counsel exists) together with appropriate IT personnel and related management.

The five steps are:

- Preservation: Complying with the duty to preserve evidence. This includes litigation hold orders, hold reminders, retaining data, and preserving related ESI.
- Collection: Gathering ESI documents necessary to respond to the subpoena. Concerns are the data map, size of the data collection, indexing the data, and collecting the data.
- Processing: Calling and preparing documents for review. Concerns de-duplication of ESI, as well as narrowing down the relevant ESI through key words, file type, data type, etc.
- Review: Categorizing and redacting documents. Documents may be categorized as relevant, privileged, or confidential. This needs attorney review.
- Production: Delivering documents to the other side. The document format (TIFF, PDF, and native platform oriented, etc.) must be decided.
- Each of the five steps entails processes and a procedure that should have been implemented prior to an LRM assessment or review. If not implemented prior to an LRM review, they need to be implemented ASAP.

21.4.1 In Order to Find All ESI, the IT Department Must Consider Its Networks, Which May Include:

- IT network
  - Network topology and content maps
  - Server/router list
  - Host servers
  - IP address

- Purpose of servers
- Work stations
- Physical locations where backup media stored
- Data storage and destruction systems and practices
- ASPs
- PDAs
- System of key players and key employees
- Accessibility/inaccessibility of records

21.4.2 An ESI Action Plan

Companies need to take the risk of ESI-based litigation seriously. Failure to do so will lead to catastrophic results. Therefore, it is suggested a company implement an action plan regarding ESI prior to litigation. If an action plan is not in place prior to litigation, it may be too late. Such plan should consider the following steps:

21.4.3 Proposed Plan

- Form a task force team to assess the current status of ESI processes within the company.
- Task force should have representatives from:
  - IT
  - Legal
  - Contract management
  - Risk management
  - Outside E-discovery counsel
- Arrange a task force meeting.
  - Review ESI rules.
  - Review status of company's past, present, and future litigation.
  - Select in-house e-discovery coordinators.
  - Review company's:
    - IT systems
    - Network topology and content maps
    - General characteristics of data

- Applicable policy intention protocols
- Focus on data storage and destruction systems and practices
- Perform inventory of company's ESI and paper records.
- Identify all types of ESI.
- Identify all obsolete unneeded records that are for reasons unknown still being preserved.
- Identify all custodians of the ESI.
- Identify all locations of all data repositories.
- Consider current IT architecture and systems to facilitate ESI retrieval and litigation holds.
- Prepare employee training program on ESI and ESI policies.
- Select two technical IT E-discovery coordinators.
- Identify and retain outside experts and E-discovery vendors:
  - Determine what outside services, if any, may be required immediately or in the foreseeable future.
  - Review experts previously used by the company.
  - Integrate experts and vendors into various tasks of the team.
- Prepare and implement a customized E-discovery litigation response plan and procedures to identify, preserve, collect, process, review, analyze, and produce ESI.
- Coordinate with outside counsel on handling all technical e-discovery issues.

A well-thought-out ESI action plan is critical to the survival of many corporations, especially those doing business in the United States. As Ralph Losey, in his book *Introduction to e-Discovery*, points out, "Today millions of British Pounds and US Dollars are being spent on e-discovery cures. This expense is a harsh reality of litigation."[2]

---

[2] Ralph Losey, *Introduction to e-Discovery*, Chicago (ABA Publishing, 2009), 16.

22

Document Management

In the previous chapters we have discussed data privacy issues facing companies as well as E-discovery risks a company faces. However, all of the issues and legal risks they pose can be considered subsets of the overall data management issue a company faces. In other words, how does a company identify, define, protect and manage its data? A document management program will, of course, also encompass E-discovery and data privacy concerns.

22.1 The Corporate Landscape

When a company considers a data and document management program, it must look at the program from the business risk and legal risk standpoints.

- Business rationale and risk: Protecting a company's most valuable asset: information—data and documents and inherent risks.
- Legal rationale and risks: Strict laws and regulation-based requirements, especially for data and document retention and inherent risks.

The two above issues are of course linked. The business issue concerns access to and the efficient use of data as well as preservation of data. Therefore, what are legal issues and accompanying risks associated with a company's business rationale for the use of data and documentation?

The legal issues and risks concern primarily data as electronic evidence.

22.2 Electronic Evidence

A company sued in the United States and perhaps elsewhere, even if handling a dispute through arbitration, will have a number of legal concerns and risks to consider, such as:

- Obligation to produce
- Court orders to produce
- Discovery obligations
- Rules governing production of data and documentation
- Penalties for nonproduction
  - Fines/penalties
  - Preclusion
  - Presumption of guilt by the jury of finder of fact
- Spoliation claims

In considering the above legal concerns over electronic documentation and data, often called ESI, or "electronically stored information," a company's efficient use of data is made problematic by virtue of the numerous platforms/locations for storage and transmission of ESI. Such platforms include:

- Desktop and laptop computers
- File and mail servers
- Databases
- Backup tapes and archival media
- PDAs
- Voice mail

- Instant messaging
- Voice-over IP

22.2.1 Magnitude of ESI

To give an idea of the problem facing a company when storing data, consider the following quote.

> "A floppy disc . . . is the equivalent of 720 typewritten pages of plain text. A CD-ROM can hold up to 325,000 typewritten pages. Large corporate computer networks create backup data measured in terabytes . . . each terabyte represents the equivalent of 500 billion typewritten pages of plain text."[1]

Risks facing a company when dealing with ESI include:

- Automated deletion of ESI over time because of volume
- Limited access to backups and legacy systems
  - Sparse
  - Cost
  - Retained knowledge
- Failure to follow rules regarding E-discovery, such as the failure to initiate a litigation "hold"

22.2.2 Legal Risk Management Objectives When Dealing with ESI

A company's primary objectives when dealing with ESI prior to litigation are:

- Handling ESI discovery obligations in a cost efficient/time efficient manner

---

[1] *Manual for Complex Litigation*, 4th ed, Sec 11.446, available on the Internet at http://www-fjc.gov/public/home.nsf/pages/470.

- Initiating required litigation "hold" requirements
- Prevention of spoliation (destruction or loss of ESI) problems or spoliation claims

22.3 ESI Requirements

To avoid fines, penalties, and even loss of litigation in the United States, a company's documentation retention program (DRP) must show the following requirements:

- A retention policy must be in place and must be followed.
- Corporate IT personnel must be involved.
- The program must allow for suspension of auto-delete programs when needed.
- Must be able to identify "key players"—interview them and preserve their ESI.
- Litigation holds must be properly issued and reissued from time to time.
- The program must create a defensible record of compliance with retention policy and litigation hold processes.

22.3.1 Litigation Hold

There are several risks and issues surrounding a litigation hold. Risks surrounding proper issuance of a litigation hold include:

- When is it triggered? The trigger of the duty to issue a litigation hold is when litigation is "reasonably likely" (i.e., it is ambiguous).
- A company must take into consideration the company's auto-delete processes. What are they?
- Communication with IT is essential.
- A company must quickly and clearly communicate to all relevant employees and vendors who provide data management the scope of the hold and importance of compliance.

22.3.2 *Duty to Locate Relevant Information:*

If a company is involved with litigation in the United States, it has a duty to locate all relevant information, data, and documents—including ESI. This can be quite onerous, as it requires:

- Familiarity with document retention policies
- Involvement with IT personnel
- Communication to "key players" of litigation hold
- Location and retrieval of all relevant information

The legal risks facing a company that fails to handle the above requirements in an economical/efficient manner can be tremendous. Companies have been sanctioned millions of dollars for failing to abide by ESI requirements or, even worse, have lost the respective lawsuits, covering even more. It is inexcusable to lose any kind of major litigation because of a lack of properly developed document management system. What can a company do to mitigate the legal risks surrounding document management to comply with US requirements?

22.4 Plan of Action

A company must take the following steps to develop an adequate data and document management plan:

- Assess the company's current use of technology documents.
- Locate all in the company's possession.
- Use technology to leverage legal requirements.
- Retain experts or outside consultants to above or to help implement systems/processes.
- Implement policies and procedures addressing all legal risks posed by ESI.

22.4.1 Risk Assessment of ESI

To implement an appropriate plan of action, a company must conduct a risk assessment of its processes and capabilities by:

- Seeking proposals of vendors (outside experts)
- A top-to-bottom analysis
  - ESI and paper documents
  - Hardware and software
  - Management of data
  - Retention of data
  - Litigation holds
  - Disaster preparedness

22.5 ESI Implementation

The legal risks facing companies in today's legal and regulatory climate, especially in the United States, are enormous. Failure to implement a data and document management program that not only addresses a company's business concerns but legal obligations as well can be disastrous. The development and implementation of an LRM program addressing these concerns is not a luxury but a necessity. It is highly recommended that a company implement a data and documentation management program that addresses ESI and all of its issues.

23

Identification of Legal Risk

23.1 Kinds of Legal Risk

Companies face many kinds of legal risks on a regular basis, depending on the company and the industry it is in. Manufacturing companies, for instance, face a number of legal risks, such as:

- Exposure from governmental noncompliance
  - Environmental
  - Regulatory
  - Antitrust
  - Immigration or visa issues
  - FTC, CPSC, EPA, DOE issues
  - Federal and state tax issues
- Litigation exposure
  - Private lawsuits
  - Product liability
- Collection claims
  - Bankruptcy claims
  - Collection-related lawsuits
  - Credit claims

- Intellectual property
  - Trade secret claims
  - Patent infringement claims
  - Copyright and trademark infringement claims
  - Employee theft of IP
  - FOSS issues
- Property issues
  - Management of real estate leases
  - Negotiation of real estate acquisition
  - Sale of property
- Contracts
  - Noncompliance
  - Government contract issues
  - Employment/labor-related issues
  - Insurance claims

The above-mentioned areas of legal risk can manifest in many ways. A merger/acquisition deal, if not properly handled, can result not only in litigation but contract claims, risky obligations, IP issues, assumption of liabilities not expected, regulatory issues, and other matters that follow with the sale of business such as tax, etc.

Most risk management books tend to lump legal risk into other categories without specifying the legal exposure that is involved. Such categories usually include:

- Product risk
- Customer risk
- Regulatory risk
- Financial risk
- Taxation risk
- Service risk
- IP risk

All of the above are of course legitimate areas of risk. However, each area contains at least an element of legal risk and exposure, if not a major legal risk component.

23.2 How to Identify Legal Risk

How do you identify potential legal risks in any corporate setting?

Obviously, legal risk can be identified through a series of legal audits using risk modeling tools, interviews, and surveys. Once potential risks or risk factors have been identified, an action plan can be put together. Only through a legal audit or review will legal risks become apparent.

In typical cases, many companies in the United States would have an HR Department. In many companies, HR is a dependent of the Law Department. In fact, it may be in charge of various employee-related matters, including pensions or 401(k) plans. An audit of HR processes, including the use of interviews and employee surveys, could identify various risks, leading to the recommendation of risk management or risk-shifting strategies.

For example, in a hypothetical scenario, if company XYZ performs a risk audit on its HR Department, the following results and recommended actions from the risk manager might result in the following:

- Audit of XYZ HR

The audit of XYZ HR has identified numerous areas of legal risk. Such areas and recommended actions to mitigate risk are as follows:

- Lack of effective partnering with XYZ Law Department:
    - Description: Critical legal issues are present in HR function. XYZ needs a process to escalate these issues to XYZ Law Department for handling.
    - Risk factors: Improper handling of sensitive issues— liabilities, investigations, fines, penalties, etc.
    - Status: Ongoing.
    - Recommended action: Develop standards and processes for escalation, handling, and control of HR legal matters.

- Employee handbook:
  - Description: The employee handbook is an important document, which communicates policies to the workforce.
  - Risk factors: Policies not communicated properly and not followed.
  - Status: Ongoing.
  - Recommended action: Review and approve XYZ Legal Department's revisions to handbook.

- Lack of training re US legal requirements:
  - Description: A US training program is needed for managers, especially for non-US citizens who rotate to other branches or offices around the world.
  - Risk factors: Liabilities, investigations, fines, penalties, private litigation, etc.
  - Status: Ongoing.
  - Recommended action: Develop and implement a US training program.

- Wage and hour issues:
  - Description: Lack of systematic characterization of job titles as "exempt" or "nonexempt."
  - Risk factors: Fines and penalties; responsibility for unpaid overtime across entire job classifications; a Department of Labor (DOL) investigation or IRS investigation could be triggered by violation.
  - Status: Ongoing.
  - Recommended action: Develop standards and process for escalation, handling and control of HR legal matters.

- ERISA audit (in the United States):
  - Description: Identified critical missing documents; lack of ERISA processes.

- Risk factors: Significant liabilities, fines, penalties, investigation by DOL and IRS.
- Status: Pending review by board of directors.
- Recommended action: Devote resources to find missing documents, implement critical processes, and create risk management plan going forward to follow ERISA regulations.

- Other issues:
  - Description: Inadequate documentation of employee discipline; lack of document retention, and lack of workplace advisory posters, etc.
  - Risk factors: Potential employee termination issues, administrative issues, fines, penalties, and litigation.
  - Status: Investigation ongoing.
  - Recommended action: Develop document retention program; order workplace advisory posters, and initiate managerial training regarding documentation of employee discipline.

- EPLI insurance program (in the US):
  - Description: Shifting legal risk of employee-related litigation to insurance company two by obtaining employee litigation insurance.
  - Action: Discussing RFPs from insurance broker in effort to obtain favorable EPLI insurance coverage.
  - Status: EPLI insurance expected in October 2013.

The above legal risks identified by XYZ's audit of its HR Department are typical of a legal risk audit. The LRM process, including legal risk shifting strategies, can be successfully used to control and mitigate legal risk. A legal risk audit should focus on those departments that frequently come into contact with employees or customers, as those departments or divisions have the most legal exposure.

24

Implementation of a Crisis Management Strategy

Any discussion of LRM would not be complete without a brief discussion of crisis management. Crisis risk management (CRM) itself would be a topic for a book. There are numerous books on the topic. Nonetheless, for purposes of this book and a LRM discussion it is a fitting topic to discuss. Without effective management of a corporate crisis, a company's future would be in doubt. Any LRM program should consider the development of a crisis management strategy for foreseeable events and the implementation of crisis risk management within the organization.

24.1 Crisis Defined

What is a crisis? A crisis can be considered to be a major unpredictable (or in some cases predictable) or catastrophic event that has potentially disastrous consequences. A crisis, in other words, is a major unpredictable event that may significantly damage or impact a company or organization by harming its brand, reputation, or public image. The problem with a "crisis" is that not only can't it always be forecast or predicted, a crisis can and will affect stakeholders, which can determine the fate of the company.

The past decade can be considered the decade of the "mega crisis." Many people have been affected (some have died) because of the crises or mega-crises that have happened. Examples include:

- Coke and Pepsi were accused of selling or manufacturing tainted products containing pesticides by an Indian NGO.
- Enron, Worldcom, and Tyco were accused of financial scandals.
- The World Trade Center towers in New York were destroyed.
- The financial and housing collapse and major recession of 2008.
- Toyota implicated in recalls because of brake issues.
- The tsunami affecting Thailand and Indonesia, resulting in deaths of approximately 250,000 people.
- The Fukushima Daiichi nuclear disaster which is still ongoing
- Major banks having their credit card customers' names stolen by computer hackers

There are numerous kinds of crises that a company should be prepared to handle, especially in an international context. Among them are financial crises, natural disasters, product failures, workplace violence, cyber-attack, or hacking, and, of course, terrorism.

It is undisputable that a major crisis can pose serious threats to a company, and, therefore, the crisis must be managed. Crises can result in (a) government fines, (b) loss of retailer confidence, (c) loss of investor confidence, (d) loss of employee confidence, and (e) massive litigation, including class actions.[1] In other words, the end of the company!

The problem facing any risk manager or in-house counsel is that the media in today's society has become very anti-business. As this anti-business culture of attack has gotten worse over the last

---

[1] Robert W. Littleton and Thomas R. Cherry, "*International Crisis Management,*" *International Corporate Practice*, Carole Basri, editor, New York: PLI 2011, 8–3.

twenty years, a crisis can no longer be handled by a simple PR or marketing statement. A full-fledged crisis management operation must be put in place. Damage control is now a very serious matter for any potential crisis, no matter how small. Today, more and more companies have to consider issues that negatively affect the company's brand and how best to counteract them.

It has been said that a company has twenty-four hours to put a strategy into place to handle a crisis. Some now say that because of the Internet, a company only has a few hours to address the situation. The impact of a company's strategy or lack thereof will probably be felt in ten to twenty days—or even less. Companies without an adequate strategy have failed to recover from the crisis. So what should a crisis management strategy consist of?

24.2 Crisis Management Strategy

Companies that successfully manage crises have used four or five basic steps to prepare for a crisis to the extent possible. They include the following steps:

- Identify the major areas of vulnerability the company faces.
- Develop an action plan for addressing actual and/or potential and unexpected threats or crisis.
- Form a crisis management team to deal with or handle threats.
- Simulate crisis scenarios of potential threats to prepare the company.
- Learn from the experience of managing the crisis.

Other companies have used a variety of steps to handle crises, including:

- Avoiding the crisis through proactive steps
- Preparing for the crisis through preparation and planning
- Properly reacting as soon as the crisis exists, and
- Resolving the crisis

To help put everything into context, a company should realize that crises, including international crises, occur in stages. The crisis management strategy should be prepared to deal with the stages as they unfold. Each stage requires certain responses from the company, and each stage has a certain impact upon a company.[2] Typically, however, a company does not have a crisis management strategy in place, especially one that can handle the various stages of a crisis. Many times a company is caught sleeping without a strategy and fails to adequately manage or resolve the crisis, which may severely impact the company. Usually, a mismanaged or badly handled crisis often follows a similar pattern:

- Early indications of a crisis starting—perhaps reports from the Service Department indicating product failure or serious defects.
- Warnings of the upcoming crisis are ignored by company management. Maybe the Service Department's warnings go unheeded by management.
- The crisis explodes, overwhelming management as deaths or serious injuries are reported due to product failure or product defects.
- Management tries to resolve the crisis quickly but without success as it failed to consider the ramifications of the crisis and how to handle it.
- The company fails to take adequate measures to handle the crisis as the crisis continues to unfold as reported by the media.
- The company suffers the consequences of an outraged media, public, and even some or all stakeholders.
- The company's existence and brand is severely threatened or put into jeopardy as its stock plummets and lawsuits are filed causing its reputation to be severely tarnished.

---

[2] Ibid, 8:4.

24.3 International Crisis

In today's world, many companies do business internationally. Because of international considerations, an international crisis is harder to manage than a domestic crisis. As it is more complex, companies caught up in an international crisis have to pay more attention to international, cultural, and communication issues than they would in a purely domestic scenario. Cross-border crisis management has become very important. Therefore, an international crisis requires a number of steps, including:

- Planning for an international crisis
- Appointing a crisis manager to handle international issues
- Establishment of a crisis management team equipped to handle international crisis
- Knowledge of foreign situations as they impact the company
- Communications
- Cross-border management of the crisis

The principle focus of any crisis management strategy, especially in an international contest, is communications. All crisis management plans call for effective crisis communications, which many times are not always executed properly. Inadequate or failed communications lead to bad publicity, unhappy stakeholders including employees, and potential disaster. An effective crisis communication strategy is necessary for any international crisis. Call in an outside crisis PR consultant if needed.

A number of processes are needed to implement an effective crisis communication strategy to manage an international crisis, including:

- Creation of the crisis communication team.
- Identify key spokespersons who will speak for the organization. Who are they? What are their roles?
- Training in relevant cultural issues, if the crisis involves other cultures.

- Establishment of communication procedures and protocols. Who communicates to whom and why?
- Identify key messages to communicate to key stakeholders and groups.
- Decide on communication methods to be used. Do they involve the Internet, TV, radio, etc? May be decided by the geographic location of the crisis.
- Effective use of social media
- Retain the use of a well respected outside Crisis PR professional
- Be ready to handle the crisis as it unfolds. Generally, if all steps have been properly implemented the company should be prepared.

24.4 Communication Components of a Crisis Management Plan

As stated above, communications is important. Therefore, a communications plan must take into consideration proper communication to numerous entities, including:

- The media
- Employees
- Crisis Management Team
- Government
- Websites
- The public
- The stakeholders (internal and external)

24.5 Considerations

When establishing a crisis management strategy, a number of questions must be asked.

- How many disputes or potential disputes are involved?
- How many participants are involved?
- How many stakeholders are involved?

- How is the best way to communicate effectively to the media and stakeholders?
- Who should the spokesperson be?
- Should Upper Management be the face of the company?
- Should there be more than one spokesperson?
- What are the facts surrounding the crisis?
- How many cultures are involved?

A company that has an effective crisis management strategy in place will be able to handle a crisis when it happens. Those companies who are not ready to handle crises or who fail to handle them properly not only will fail to prosper but may also fail.

25

Crisis Management: Hypothetical Case in Point

Cell phone disaster

PanStar is the newest cell phone company in country X and the fastest growing cell phone company in the world. Its hit cell phone, the "Cinnamon Stick," has sold five million units in India, its largest market. It has sold two million units in country X and has sold three million units in the United States, its second-largest market. Its annual sales for 2012 exceeded $75 million US. Not bad for a start-up.

As a new start-up company, PanStar depended on venture capital. It found financing with a US venture capital company—the Equity Venture Capital Group (EVCG) in New York. EVCG has invested $25 million in the start-up and was in the process of providing another loan of $25 million to finance expansion. Soon PanStar would list itself on its country's stock exchange. It could then expand to other countries. The CEO of EVCG, Mr. Overby, was very happy about EVGC's investment and thought the loan would be available by September 1.

On May 1, 2011, President Park was informed by Mr. Kho, his head engineer, that several faulty battery chargers were found, which could cause the cell phone battery to overheat.

The problem was isolated and identified to the faulty manufacture of the battery chargers by PanStar's main subcontractor, I-Risk, located in Mongolia. It appeared only a few faulty battery chargers were sold and I-Risk thought it had corrected the problem. No problem was expected, as only a few faulty battery chargers were produced, and overheating was usually not that serious.

On July 1, 2011, President Park received a frantic phone call from his major distributor in India, Mr. Raj Samsoran. He had received word that one of the cell phones had just exploded, killing the cell phone owner, a boy of twelve years of age in New Delhi. He promised to look into it ASAP!

On July 2, President Park was informed that the Indian Product Safety Commission was outraged over the cell phone explosion and was blaming PanStar. It wanted to immediately ban the sale of all PanStar cell phones in India. It called for an official investigation of the alleged incident. It also wanted to impose fines.

On July 3, Mr. Overby of EVGC called President Park about the Indian cell phone situation. Obviously, if the cell phone batteries were defective, it may be hard to get financing. EVGC was starting to question PanStar's products. Was investing in PanStar a good idea? Should it provide the loan or not?

On July 4, a reporter from a local TV station contacted PanStar's PR Department wanting to interview President Park about the "exploding" cell phones. A TV station from the United States wanted to interview him as well. So did an Indian TV station.

July 5, President Park knew he had to act fast if he wanted to handle the crisis. Otherwise, the company faced ruin. He called in his management team—his head of communications; his head of Sales, his VP of operations, his head Service safety engineer, and his CFO. He asked for advice. What steps should be taken with the following in mind:

- What steps should be taken by the crisis management team to resolve the crisis?

- What steps should the Communications Department take, if any, regarding the crisis?
- Are there any international issues that should be addressed? If so, what are they?
- What stakeholders are affected by the crisis and how should their concerns be addressed?

SUMMARY

As LRM should be used proactively to reduce the threat of legal risk, a company needs to think of strategies that can be used prior to litigation to reduce risk. Such strategies that can be used include the implementation of a compliance program, creation of a records retention program, use of an e-mail management program, implementation of an e-discovery policy or process, a data management program, and the creation of a crisis management process.

The use of a compliance program can be an effective risk management tool. A compliance program, if properly implemented, will not only increase a company's brand image but will reinforce ethical behavior among the employees, which has positive benefits. This, in turn, helps minimize legal risk and exposure.

One of the principle reasons a corporation faces legal exposure is its failure to manage information, whether in hard-copy form or in electronic form. Electronically stored information (ESI) poses numerous problems, as it is hard to manage. Not only should a company implement an information retention policy, but it should also address issues caused by ESI, including e-mail issues.

E-discovery issues, if left unchecked, may result in enormous costs and expenses if a company fails to implement an E-discovery policy, especially if it faces litigation in the United States. It is very important for a company as part of its LRM program to implement an E-discovery plan that can mitigate exposure to costs, fees, and expenses.

Notwithstanding the implementation of a compliance program, a crisis management strategy needs to be in place. A CRM program is becoming more important as an LRM tool because of the numerous media attacks and/or culture of attack in which most businesses operate in today's environment.

PART 4

Legal Risk Management and Litigation

Though a company may have implemented legal risk mitigation, avoidance, or even LRM shifting strategies and processes, there will come a point where litigation, especially in the United States, is inevitable. Though pre-litigation risk management strategies are vital to minimize the exposure of litigation risks, managing litigation properly is essential for a satisfactory outcome. Companies that fail to properly manage outside litigation face potential out-of-control lawyers and out-of-control legal fees and costs. Also, if not properly handled, any failure to hire law firm based on a comprehensive plan will result in lack of coordination, little continuity, lack of consistency, and even separate law firms taking contradictory positions when dealing with different divisions. Sometimes corporations rush to hire lawyers based on areas of expertise without looking past a short-term objective. A company that fails to optimize its use of legal support services ends up hiring numerous law firms for numerous areas such as tax, customs, litigation, employment, etc. This results in increased costs, and chances for successful resolution of litigation or commercial disputes may disappear. Therefore, this section of the book stresses basic litigation management concepts, as that is also of utmost importance.

2 6

Corporate Structure Issues

Companies, especially multinational companies or conglomerates with several subsidiaries, can effectively mitigate risk through the use of a holding company. The creation of a corporate structure that uses a holding company can limit and isolate liability and legal risk arising from the operations of individual subsidiaries. This is especially true of companies doing business in the United States through subsidiaries or multiple operations.

26.1 Holding Company: Liability Containment

US corporations generally have liability limited to their assets, and stockholders are not personally liable for the debts of the corporation. A US corporation is generally subject to suit in the United States only in the state of its incorporation and in states where it does business. These principal features of the US corporation generally result in containment of the liability for that corporation's debts or acts to the corporation itself without attribution of liability up the corporate chain of ownership.

The prospect of enormous punitive damage awards against corporations by American juries and the possible imposition of large civil fines alone demonstrate the need for maintaining corporate formalities and utilizing a holding company structure that cuts off liability at the subsidiary level. The holding company structure isolates and confines liability to the subsidiary. The presence of one or more US holding companies between the subsidiary and the ultimate foreign parent serves as a further buffer to protect the parent from liability exposure in the United States. A related, but equally important, limited liability strategy centers on the foreign parent. Specifically, to protect its own assets, it should avoid direct US contacts so it is not subject to the jurisdiction of courts in the United States. Rather, business should be conducted through its subsidiaries.

26.2 Centralized Management of Regulatory Matters Applicable to Subsidiaries and the Group or Parent as a Whole

Many regulatory and compliance matters are measured or regulated on a controlled group basis. Since the activities of any entity down the ownership chain can affect the whole group or ultimate parent organization, usually certain elements of control reside at the holding company. This precludes "stray" arrangements from being adopted on an ad hoc basis. As required, the holding company can access information generally not available to various group members.

The holding company can put together more effective arrangements (e.g., master contacts) for use by group members to obtain the best terms. Immigration can also be effectively managed by a single source as opposed to numerous conflicting sources.

Centralized management of regulatory matters applicable to subsidiaries also has other benefits, such as the followings.

26.2.1 Tax Planning and Minimization

The holding company structure offers the benefit of centralized planning and control over US tax liabilities. Considerations include the following:

- Consolidating country and group management and reporting
- Federal tax
- State and local taxes
- Excise, property, and other taxes

26.2.2 Holding Company Structure Promotes Efficiency and Minimizes Redundancy in Certain Areas, thereby Generating Cost Savings, to the Extent Centralized Services Are Provided to the Entire Group

- Legal
- Risk management and insurance
- Other administrative efficiencies provision (i.e., specialized legal services to group companies)

26.2.3 Holding Company Structure Facilitates Synergies and Efficiencies between Subsidiaries and Operating Groups through Knowledge Sharing

- Transfer of technology
- People mobility
- Teaming on projects
- Shared services
- Employee benefits
- Insurance

26.2.4 Risk Mitigation through a Holding Company

As part of an LRM plan, companies need to consider the holding company structure, especially in the United States. A holding company structure can promote the centralized management of risk mitigation and promote the ease of transfer or sale of assets, if necessary.

With the recent explosion of adverse liability judgments against foreign companies in the United States, especially in product liability areas, it is in the best interests of corporate conglomerates to effectively limit their liability through a holding company structure. Obviously, limiting a potentially onerous judgment to a subsidiary would be a desirable goal of the corporate parent.

26.3 Potential Issues Involving Holding Companies

The use of a holding company structure in the United States is not without its drawbacks. Among the drawbacks are:

- Taxes on a state level
- Costs of running a holding company structure
- Proper corporate formalities must be followed

26.3.1 Legal Significance of the Corporate Structure

One of the major features of a corporate organization in the United States is that it insulates shareholders from personal liability for the debts of the corporation. Therefore, under normal conditions, a corporate parent will not be held liable for the obligations of its subsidiary. The court will not impose liability upon a parent for the obligations of its subsidiary in the absence of compelling legal reasons. However, under certain circumstances courts will hold the parent or stockholders liable. It will, in other words, "pierce the corporate veil" and go past the subsidiary and hold the parent liable. The major legal doctrine allowing the courts to do this are set forth below.

- Fraud

If a subsidiary is being used by the parent as a vehicle to perpetuate a fraud or crime.

- Alter ego

If there is such a close relationship between the parent and the subsidiary that the former may be said to be the "alter ego" of the latter.

Though fraud is usually not a major concern of conglomerates, the alter ego doctrine can be. Courts will sometimes treat a wholly owned subsidiary as an instrumentality of the parent, hence alter ego if the parent fails to respect corporate formalities necessary for the proper formation and function of a subsidiary.

Therefore, if the parent exerts too much control over a subsidiary, and the subsidiary does not follow corporate formalities, an alter ego situation can exist.

To determine if an alter ego situation exists, courts will look at a number of factors indicating control, such as:

- Stock ownership
- Officers and directors
- Financing
- Responsibility of day-to-day operations
- Arrangements for payment of salaries
- Whether the parent corporation uses the property of the subsidiary as its own
- Minimum compliance of general corporate law

A court may be inclined to invoke the alter ego doctrine if it finds a subsidiary disregards minimum corporate formalities.

Specifically, corporations in the United States are required to hold annual stockholder meetings, elect officers, annually file a franchise tax return, maintain separate corporate minute books, and maintain separate accounting records. Failure to follow these processes can result in a court holding that the subsidiary is merely the alter ego of the parent.

To avoid this, the holding company needs to do the following:

- Maintain separate corporate records for each subsidiary.
- Segregate the funds of each subsidiary.
- Maintain separate books of account for each subsidiary.
- Assure each subsidiary is properly charged for the centralized service provided by the holding company.
- Keep all minute books up to date.

27

Use of Outside Counsel

When using outside counsel, most companies, especially those that have affiliates or subsidiaries, need a comprehensive approach. Unfortunately, many companies hire law firms on a case-by-case or ad hoc basis. Sometimes divisions of the same company hire different law firms without thinking about potential issues of legal talent and failure to obtain high-quality legal services on a consistent and reasonably priced basis.

If a company has an in-house Law Department, it is incumbent on the in-house Law Department to develop processes to select and use outside counsel on a consistent basis with a focus on quality, reasonable fees, and, of course, success. Such success is normally the result of a long-term relationship in which outside counsel becomes a member of the company's "team," learns the business, and can, therefore, provide timely legal and business advice.

If a company does not have an in-house counsel, it must look toward retaining a law firm, which in essence acts as an in-house counsel. In other words, the law firm becomes an "outside general counsel." By hiring an outside general counsel, a company obtains a firm that can consistently and responsibly evaluates legal issues, decide how to handle them, and implement a comprehensive legal strategy.

The concept is analogous to a building contractor. Just like a building contractor knows the overall status of a building, the outside general counsel knows the complete legal requirements of his client. When a building contractor does not have the expertise to build part of the building, he calls in a subcontractor. Likewise, when legal services outside the area of expertise of the outside general counsel are required, he recommends that another law firm be retained to handle special or specific matters.

27.1 Centralization

A company either has in-house counsel or it does not. To successfully handle legal issues facing most companies these days (especially those involving litigation and the legal process), the use of outside counsel must be centralized. If a company has many divisions or subsidiaries, a department should be empowered to oversee all legal matters. There are numerous advantages to centralization of outside counsel or the legal function:

27.1.1 Advantages of Centralization

- One organization has an overview of all legal issues confronting the company and can properly advise management on legal issues.
- Efficiency: Whether in-house or outside, efficient and fast response to legal issues is necessary.
- Use of a single law firm as outside general counsel can result in monetary savings.
- Centralization of legal services lends itself to the centralization of the company's legal records, documentation, and information, creating a more efficient process.
- Centralization of legal services allows for a more efficient review of data, resulting in the proper use of information and development of an appropriate strategy.
- Investment: Whether a company is large or small, it needs to look at use of outside counsel as an investment. Picking

the right outside counsel and developing a long-term relationship with such counsel will pay dividends in the long run.

Efficient and timely use of outside legal services, whether such use of outside legal services is picked by an in-house lawyer or by a company manager or officer, relies on whether outside counsel is the right fit for the company. There are many law firms around, but not all are the right fit. Picking the right law firm or outside counsel depends on a number of factors. Many times a company picks a law firm because of a personal relationship between a company officer and a lawyer in the firm. Or maybe the firm has done a good job in advertising. The trouble is, without going through a process to determine the acceptability of a law firm, picking outside counsel can be hit or miss.

28

Picking the Law Firm: The Value Added Proposition

Whether the company is large or small and whether it has an in-house Law Department or not, picking the right outside law firm is essential. This is especially true if the company does not have in-house lawyers and opts to pick an outside general counsel. There are many law firms to pick from. But only a few really can add value and really benefit the company. The company or organization needs to ask various questions when looking for law firms that can add value.

- Does the law firm understand my business or is it willing to try and understand my business?
- Is the law firm willing to operate like a "building contractor" and let me know if other specialized law firms (subcontractors) are needed?
- Is the law firm willing to make a commitment to my company by becoming a "partner"?
- If I am picking an outside general counsel, does the firm have general, broad capabilities to handle my issues, and if so is the firm willing to "audit" the legal processes of my operations?

- Can the company or its in-house lawyers work comfortably with the outside law firms? Will they help me for the long term?
- Is the law firm willing to work with the company managers on a regular basis?
- Will the law firm, operating as an outside general counsel, be willing to interview and select other outside law firms on select matters, if needed?
- Will the law firm be willing to become a go-to law firm by offering reasonably priced solutions to my legal problems, such as using a blended rate or success fee, or do the partners think they can all charge $1,000 per hour?

In other words, is the law firm willing to become your partner? Will it invest significant resources in becoming your go-to law firm? Will it add value?

28.1 Finding Law Firms

Before a company or a company's in-house lawyers can pick the right outside law firm, a search for the right firm must be conducted. This entails a process more sophisticated than just looking at legal advertisements in the newspaper or on TV. Several tools are useful in helping find appropriate law firms and lawyers. These tools or procedures can assist most companies in finding the right firm if implemented.

First, however, a company has to assess it needs and decide what kind of firm it wants. Does it want a large firm that can handle most issues or a boutique small firm that specializes in one area of law? It could want a medium-sized regional firm that can handle many issues but does not have offices in every major city, yet has a large regional presence. Regional firms can be very cost effective when dealing with certain issues.

On the other hand, Kevin Quinley, in his book on litigation management points out that large law firms have many advantages in that sheer size of the firm will guarantee there are enough lawyers that can handle most cases.[1] Therefore, if a company has many or very serious lawsuits requiring a large team or staff of lawyers and legal assistants, a large firm is best. So if General Motors is sued in a class action over faulty brakes, etc., a large firm is best equipped to handle that kind of litigation.

Be that as it may, larger firms are not always the best answer. Smaller firms, including regional ones, will many times be more flexible when it comes to billing and perhaps be more responsive, especially when the matter is not major litigation. Small or regional firms may provide more personalized service tailored to a specific client. I would use regional firms if possible, as such firms are usually cheaper and provide a similar quality of service—sometimes even better quality—as do the large firms. However, sometimes it is best to use a national or large firm, or even a multinational law firm if there are international issues and concerns involved.

Large firms tend to have more resources to handle large and complex matters but have, like any large organization, certain processes and procedures that may not allow them to operate as cheaply and efficiently as smaller firms. Large firms often have a bureaucracy that renders them less flexible and nimble than a small or regional firm. However, as large firms tend to have more offices and more lawyers, it may be advantageous to use these firms when the scope of litigation or the seriousness of the matter requires such resources. So, as stated above, before picking a law firm, a company must assess its legal requirements. Is it "bet the farm" litigation or a less serious matter? Does it require a national or international presence, or is the matter isolated to a smaller geographic area?

28.2 Thoughts on Selecting the Appropriate Law Firm

There are a number of things a company can do to pick the best firm for its legal matters if it does not have a GC. Some of them are discussed below.

---

[1] Kevin M Quinley, *Litigation Management*, Dallas: International Risk Management Institute (1995), p 9

- Ask around the industry. What law firms, if any, represent or have represented similar companies in the industry?
- Industry or trade journals—even newspapers—may mention firms that are familiar with the industry.
- Law firms maintain websites that contain information about the firm and its abilities. A search on the Internet may list firms with lawyers that have a specialty you are looking for.
- What does the local business community say about the particular law firm? What do your peers or colleagues say?
- If you have used a law firm in the past for a different matter, maybe it can recommend a firm, if needed.
- What firm or firms do your colleagues recommend, if any?
- If you have an outside general counsel, that firm should handle the matter.

Once you have located three or four firms, set up a meeting. Not only do you want a firm that can handle your matter, but you need a firm or a partner at a firm that you trust and are comfortable with. To find the best firm and/or partner, you should ask a number of questions regarding the firm and, more specifically, the partner. In essence, conduct a reference check on the law firm. I would suggest the following questions:

- What kind of billing arrangements does the firm expect? Does the partner bill by the hour or on a project basis? Or both?
- Staffing: How will the partner staff the case?
- How busy is the partner? Can he take the case?
- Will the firm pay enough attention to your case?
- What experience does the firm and/or partner have in dealing with cases such as yours?
- How committed is the firm to you? Does it want to enter into a long term relationship?

At the end, prior to picking the firm, you have to ask yourself:

> Am I impressed with the firm and, more importantly, am I comfortable or impressed with the partner or lead attorney with which I met? Can I work with them? Do I trust them with my legal problem or lawsuit?

When a company retains a law firm to handle a specific matter, it can lead to a long and perhaps expensive relationship. This is especially true in the USA, where USA stands for "You Sue Anyone"! It is imperative, then, to find a firm that can not only efficiently handle the legal matter at hand, but one that has the best interests of the company at heart. Can the firm add value to your case? What is the firm's value add?

What I recommend at the end of the selection process, when you have narrowed down your search to one or two firms you like, is to conduct a reference check. Do not be afraid to ask the law firms for a list of former clients. Contact the clients, if possible, and ask them how satisfied they were with the firm. The law firm may think it did a great job for the client, but, in fact, the client may have a different opinion of the firm's abilities or a different opinion of the partner in question. A reference check often helps uncover issues regarding the firm's services, but it is not guaranteed. Still, it is a method that may at least help you satisfy any open questions you may have and help you make a decision as to which firm to use. Remember to pick the firm you are most comfortable with.

29

US litigation

The main issue facing companies involved in U.S. litigation is that U.S. litigation compared to litigation in many other countries is quite unique and expensive. U.S. litigation is not only complex but can be quite costly, onerous, and burdensome. The key element of U.S. litigation is that it is notice-based pleading in a common law setting, which means the facts of cases are to be developed through a complex discovery process in which lawyers for the parties play an adversarial role. Unlike in many countries, courts in the U.S. usually act as more of an umpire and will let the attorneys for both sides actively and aggressively handle the case.

29.1 Discovery

Discovery, by its very nature, takes up time, adds a great deal of expense to the cost of litigation (for both parties) and can lead to the disruption of business.

The kinds of discovery vary but are primarily limited to the following formats:

- Depositions
  - Oral examination

184 | *Bryan E. Hopkins*

- • May involve written questions
- • May involve key employees and/or officers of the company
- • Interrogatories
  - • Answers to written questions posed by the other side
- • Production of documents and things and entry upon land for inspection and other purposes
- • Production of ESI
- • Physical examination of the evidence

It has been noted that discovery in the United States is like no other discovery process elsewhere. The United States, in fact, provides litigants a much greater ability to review all broadly relevant documents than any other jurisdiction in the world. The expense, delay, and business disruption associated with US discovery are unparalleled.[1]

29.2 Jury Trials

The USA, unlike most civil law jurisdictions, uses a jury system for civil proceedings. That means a jury comprised of six to twelve people from the surrounding area will decide the facts of the matter in question, effectively deciding the outcome of the case. The judge acts basically as an umpire by deciding legal questions. The problem this presents is that a group of ordinary laypeople from the area will decide the outcome of the case, no matter how technical or difficult it is.

The fact that a jury will decide the outcome of the case adds an element of unpredictability. Regardless of how strong the evidence is, a jury verdict is never guaranteed. Litigants, whether the plaintiff or defendant, often decide to settle, regardless of the strength of the merits of the claim or defense to the claim due to unpredictability, the cost and expense of trial, the potential disruption to business, and the negative publicity.

---

[1] Donovan, Donald F., *"Introducing Foreign Clients to U.S. Civil Litigation"*, *International Litigation Strategies and Practice*, Barton Legum, editor, Chicago: American Bar Association, 2005, 34.

29.3 Absence of Fee-Shifting Statutes

Unlike many countries, the United States does not usually have fee-shifting statutes allowing the prevailing party to shift its legal fees and expenses to the losing party. Each party to a litigation bears his or her own legal expenses unless a statute or contractual agreement provides that the prevailing party should be awarded attorneys' fees. Courts usually refuse to award attorney fees to the prevailing party in absence of such contractual stipulation or statutes.

The absence of fee shifting, in most cases, is extremely important. The prevailing party in litigation may very well lose financially if the amount awarded at trial does not exceed the cost of litigation. This combined with the other costly factors of litigation, such as discovery, creates a litigation system that is more costly, time consuming, and burdensome than most litigation systems in other countries. Just because a party wins or prevails at trial in the U.S. doesn't mean the party will win financially. Be careful about litigation in the U.S.

29.4 Strategy

In the case where parties are unable to resolve the dispute prior to litigation, a litigant must develop a winning trial strategy. In the U.S. such strategy will be based on complex rules of evidence allowing or disallowing the admission of certain evidence, including testimony or documents, etc. The parties will obviously try to position themselves to be in the strongest position possible up to and during the trial, regardless of whether an out-of-court settlement is finally reached. What does this trial strategy mean to most litigants? It means :

- Loss of time.
- Expense.
- Potential interruption of business.
- The cost and expense of business interruption.

- Potential bad or negative publicity.
- Negative impact on the company's brand image
- Potential loss of reputation.
- In the United States, trials are public. Does the public exposure of a trial matter to you?
- As trials are public, the media often plays a part in reporting and influencing the case. Do you want this?

29.5 Class Actions

Another unique aspect of US litigation is that of class actions. In the United States, groups of claimants are able to sue as a class. Such litigation is called a "class action," and it exposes corporate defendants to potential life-threatening litigation where enough class members are involved. A class action could consist of thousands of claimants represented by one claimant. If a company is sued in a class action, it is potentially exposed to a jury award in the millions of dollars. Another issue is that there could be more than one class action or multiple class actions in a number of states. The potential legal exposure and high transactions costs of numerous trials are great. Class actions have in fact led to the destruction of companies and have forced certain manufacturing industries to leave the U.S. marketplace.

29.6 LRM: US Litigation

To properly manage civil litigation in the United States, companies need to implement LRM strategies and processes by either creation of an in-house Law Department or a Risk Management Department that is capable of overseeing or managing outside litigation. Depending on the legal exposure of a company, it can be a full-time job. This management function will be key in properly coordinating litigation to avoid excessive costs, duplication of effort, and minimization of disruptions to a company's business, as well as setting an effective trial strategy.

What many foreign companies doing business in the United States fail to appreciate is that an outside litigation lawyer does not necessarily have the company's best interests in mind during litigation. A litigator wants to win, regardless of the cost. Many companies have paid millions of dollars to law firms during litigation when a resolution to the dispute was available had the parties tried to actively settle the case. Remember, a trial lawyer's business is trial work and not settlement.

An in-house legal manager or risk manager, representing the company's best interests, can help facilitate settlement once a legal risk assessment as to the validity, cost, and expense of litigation is made. In fact, during trial, a settlement is still possible and can be facilitated by in-house counsel or risk management. Therefore, the Law Department or the appropriate risk manager (if no Law Department exists) or controller should maintain control and oversight of any litigation. A LRM program can be very helpful in managing the legal risk process as well as providing litigation oversight.

29.6.1 Reasons for an Internal Legal Risk Management Process

Companies facing U.S. litigation are often exposed to excessive fees and costs, massive business disruption, lengthy litigation, and the unpredictability of the jury system. Though, obviously, outside litigation counsel is necessary in most cases, an in-house Law Department can save the company great sums of money by managing the litigation process. Such management involves the assessment, management, and potential transfer of risk through various LRM strategies, including:

- Effective coordination of legal defense efforts in order for the company to avoid duplication of costs and effort from case to case
- Coordination of witnesses, answers and interrogatory responses, documents, and depositions

- Acting as the central site for all facts, positions, decisions on legal issues, and motions
- Development, implementation, and coordination of a defense plan

30

Legal Fees and Costs

A company, wherever situated, will eventually be subject to litigation, government investigations, fines, employee actions, etc. To properly defend itself will require the use of law firms, especially in the United States. However, as explained in the preceding chapter, legal fees and costs can be excessive. The financial well-being of a company may depend upon how well it is able to manage outside legal fees and costs.

As part of an overall LRM program, a company's Law Department must implement processes to control, reduce, and manage outside legal fees and costs. By utilizing legal risk management tools, a Law Department or Risk Management Department can proactively reduce legal fees and costs.

30.1 Tools for Reducing Legal Fees

- Processes that can measure the performance of outside counsel
- Processes that track legal costs and expenses
- Use of KPIs that measure the Law Departments metrics
- Creation of a contract management system, which standardizes contracts and forms

- Negotiation of legal fee agreements with outside counsel
- Use of outside billing guidelines, which prevent excessive billing by law firms

30.1.1 KPIs

Key performance indexes (KPIs) are an effective way to measure a Law Department's metrics as well as use and effectiveness of outside counsel. I recommend a corporate Law Department to establish at least ten to twenty KPI metrics to get a good picture of the effectiveness of not only the Law Department but outside counsel. This can be reflected in the dashboard on your computer monitor. Typical examples would be:

- Law Department's total expense
- Law Department's total expense as a percentage of revenue
- Number of active litigation matters
- Number of new litigation matters
- Number of closed litigation matters
- Law Department's fees for outside counsel
- Total external spending on litigation matter
- Cycle time to resolve claims
- Estimated dollar savings through use of legal risk management tools
- Percentage of legal matters that receive a management—specific post-mortem review

There are other KPIs to use, but the above metrics can be used to help quantify the number of litigation matters, average time to resolve matters, total legal costs, and savings through LRM processes. The more processes put in place to measure performance from a risk management point of view the better. KPIs not only measure the effectiveness and efficiency of a law department but can be used as a tool to improve the effectiveness of the Law Department.

31

Litigation: Hypothetical Case in Point

The Gold Connection

Five-Star Electronics began selling the GoldBug stove in its home territory of the country of Albanon in 2011. In March 2012, the CEO of Five-Star Electronics decided to sell the product in country XXX. The GoldBug stove heats gold ions, killing bacteria. Some said it was a good disinfectant and would also kill bacteria in stoves—maybe even severe acute respiratory syndrome, or SARS.

Prior to this, Five-Star, in conjunction with outside experts, consulted with the XXX Environmental Protection Agency (XXX EPA) and state regulatory bodies to get a determination on whether the stove needed to be registered in XXX as a pesticide or simply classified as a pesticide device. If it was only a pesticide device, no XXX federal registration would be required. If the Gold was classified as a pesticide and not a pesticide device, GoldBug would come under EPA regulations in XXX. Once under EPA regulations, others might also take notice about the "gold" issue, which could impact sales in those countries as well.

The XXX EPA made a determination that the stove was a device and didn't require registration. Five-Star thought it was in the clear. Mr. Kim, CEO and president of Five-Star XXX, told his

VP of sales (Mr. Smith) to ready the launch of the product in the XXX market. If successful in XXX, they would sell it in Mexico and in Canada. It was expected to be a big success and propel Five-Star to the top of the home appliance market in XXX.

Mr. Smith ordered his marketing team, under the supervision of its director, Mr. Walsh, to start a marketing campaign. Without consulting with Five-Star's Law Department, the marketing campaign was begun. After all, the EPA approved it, right? What could go wrong?

On May 12, Five-Star received news that several state EPA agencies opposed the classification of the stove as a pesticide device and thought it was a pesticide. Several environmental watchdog groups, such as Those Against Gold (TAG), began pressuring the state agencies to review the state classification. The state agencies began pressuring the EPA to change its position. Mr. Smith heard about the state EPA agencies but opted to do nothing, thinking the matter would go away.

On June 1, Five-Star was informed that the EPA changed its position on the GoldBug stove and would now require registration of the machine as a pesticide. The registration process could take more than a year, during which time Five-Star would not be able to sell any units. President Kim was told by his boss, the CEO of the parent company, Mr. Park, to "solve it." Too much money was at stake. In fact the GoldBug factory could shut down. And besides, the competition was coming out with its new and improved stove soon. Something had to be done.

On June 15, Mr. Smith met with his marketing team behind closed doors. Perhaps he screwed up when he failed to talk to the Law Department. The Law Department would be very upset if it found out what had happened. Luckily, Mr. Smith was told by Mr. Walsh that his nephew knew a district officer of the EPA. Maybe they could resolve the matter prior to getting legally involved and spending money to handle the matter. They decided to contact Mr. Walsh's nephew. Maybe they could work out a deal. Perhaps if they didn't do anything, the EPA would let them sell the washing machine, or at worst maybe pay a simple fine.

On June 30, Mr. Walsh's nephew put a call in to his friend at the EPA, Mr. Black. What could be done? Could they negotiate a deal? Mr. Black was not very sympathetic. He had been told by his boss to take a tough stand against gold infringers. Because Five-Star had not done anything to resolve the issue until now, the EPA was contemplating bringing an "agency action" against TriStar. The fine could be $5 million.

Unable to resolve the issue, Mr. Smith went to his in house lawyer and explained the dilemma. Mr. Smith was told by his lawyer they were looking at fines of over 5 million US dollars. The main problem was that Five-Star, in an effort to grab market share, already had signed a 100 million US dollar supply agreement with its most favorite customer, Acme Electronics. Acme Electronics had already advertised the product and had placed advertisements in the local circulars and local newspapers. The store had made room on its floor for the new GoldBug stove.

To make matters worse, Acme Electronics decided not to buy similar products from the competition. It was too late for Acme Electronics to cover its losses if it could not take shipment of the GoldBug.

It was obvious they had to come up with a strategy to resolve the current dispute(s). What dispute resolution strategies should they consider and why?

- Who are the parties to the dispute?
- What dispute resolution mechanisms were used?
- If litigation is used, how expensive would it be?
- If litigation was used, where would the litigation be brought?
- If litigation was used, how would XXX pick a law firm and how would it control outside legal costs?

32

Management of Outside Counsel

32.1 Cost Containment Strategies

Form: Outside Billing Guidelines—see Appendix B

Law firms charge different rates for different legal issues. Fees charged for an acquisition will be different than fees charged for litigation. The issue facing an internal law department, risk manager, or corporate manager in general, when charged with the task of managing outside firms, is, of course, management of fees and costs in relation to the legal matter being handled by the law firm. Law firms, as service providers, can get out of control if not properly managed. There are many horror stories involving excessive billing by law firms.

I remember a case involving a well-known multinational law firm that issued its unsuspecting poor client an invoice for $250,000 without any explanation of the services provided. The invoice simply said "For Services Rendered—$250,000." The client was obviously shocked. How do you go to your CFO or CEO with invoice in hand and ask that the company pay it? What will accounting say? There are numerous ways to contain and control costs. One of the major strategies in which a company can control costs is through the use of outside billing guidelines.

32.2 Outside Billing Guidelines

More and more in-house Law Departments are requiring this use when providing legal services. Most guidelines set forth basic principles that a law firm must follow, such as:

- A description of services
- What a proper invoice should look like
- When the law firm should invoice the company
- What services can be invoiced
- What a firm cannot invoice for, such as legal research, copying fees, postal fees, or work done by junior associates

Firms normally like to bill excessive fees for their young associates just out of law school. Most young associates bring little or no value to a project except the ability to do basic research. In essence, firms try to train their young associates while billing clients. This has been the standard practice for many years. But why should you have to pay for that? It is recommended that you refuse to pay for any work done by a junior associate if that associate has recently graduated from law school and has not been sufficiently trained to handle basic issues. Control your costs!

Another way law firms bill excessively is overusing the "team" concept. Many legal matters require a team of several lawyers, such as a partner who oversees a matter; a senior associate, who does most of the research and writing; and perhaps an expert in certain areas. However, on complex matters such as litigation, many law firms love to create large teams consisting of many lawyers who bill on issues regardless of adding any value. Be on guard for firms to try and overuse the "team" concept. Billing guidelines should stress that a company or its in-house Law Department must approve the lawyers a law firm wishes to put on the team.

A number of issues the outside billing guidelines should address to avoid excessive fees and costs are:

- Requirement of a case plan and budget

- A proposed strategy for handling the case
- Identification of significant activity the outside law firm expects
- A discovery end date and anticipated trial date
- Requirement that the firm gets approval from the company before filing motions
- Requirement that the law firm justify staffing
- Refusal to pay for summer associates or interns

32.3 Monthly Reporting

Not only should companies require law firms to invoice in accordance with billing guidelines set by the company, but they should also require the firm to report exactly what it did on a monthly basis. By demanding monthly reports from a firm, it is possible to get a monthly narrative on the exact services provided. This helps not only put the services a law firm has provided in perspective but can help a company question unreasonable invoices. Was the hundred-page memorandum of law on anti-trust issues necessary when a five-page executive summary would have been more practical?

Remember, unless managed properly, a law firm can easily exceed its proposed budget. It must be held accountable to a reasonable budget and not be allowed to charge excessive fees and costs. It is up to the company to manage fees and costs. It is up to you!!

33

Use of Negotiations

33.1 What Are Negotiations?

Negotiations are an often underutilized LRM tool. Used as a dispute resolution mechanism, negotiations can be used to resolve disputes, internal and external to a corporation, prior to such disputes turning into litigation. It is another tool to avoid the risk of litigation or arbitration and can minimize legal costs and expenses that might otherwise occur.

Negotiations can be simple or complex, depending on the subject matter. International negotiations are the most complex as they involve different cultures, languages, legal systems, and viewpoints. Nonetheless, all negotiations, whether domestic or international, will involve strategies, knowledge of the facts and issues, an understanding of the other side's viewpoints, and, above all else, an understanding of the problems and risks at hand.

33.2 Stages of Negotiations

Negotiation can be defined primarily as a decision-making process whereby two or more parties resolve their disputes or differences by advancing their interests vis-à-vis each other. Negotiations may be broken down into several distinct stages:

- The beginning or pre-negotiation stage
- The middle or negotiation stage
- The final or post—negotiation stage

All three stages are crucial to successful resolution of a dispute or potential dispute that could lead to the risk of litigation.

Let's discuss each stage with a few examples.

33.2.1 The Pre-negotiation Stage

Prior to negotiating with the other party or disputant, a party must understand the facts, identify the issues involved, and map out a strategy to deal with negotiations. Though it may seem easy, this stage actually involves numerous steps. Each step may involve several processes or sub-processes as well. The basic steps are as follows:

- Determining the problem at hand
- Determining the interests of all parties involved
- Identifying possible solutions
- Deciding upon negotiation strategies
- Understanding your best alternative to a negotiated agreement—sometimes called the BATNA, first coined by Roger Fisher in his book on negotiation[1]

Knowing your BATNA sets the bottom floor of any deal, as it will set the range of a possible settlement. No party will agree to

---

[1]   See Roy Lewicki, Bruce Barry and David M Saunders, *Negotiations*, NY: McGraw-Hill, 2010, p 10 which discusses BATNA as set forth in the book by Roger Fisher, William Ury, and Bruce Patton, *Getting to Yes: Negotiating Agreement without Giving In*, 2nd ed, (Penguin, 1991).

a negotiation that offers less than the party's BATNA. By way of example:

BATNA—ABC Company

Tristar wants to enter into a supply contract with ABC Company to sell TVs at 15 percent above margin. ABC wants to purchase TVs at 5 percent above margin. Tristar knows it can sell all of its TVs to Best Bros. Company at 12 percent above margin. Tristar's BATNA is 12 percent above margin.

Once a party understands the facts, has defined the dispute to be resolved, and knows its BATNA, it needs to develop its negotiation strategy. There are two basic strategies negotiators use in negotiating dispute:

- Position based
- Interest based

33.2.2 Competitive-Style (Position-Based) Negotiation

Negotiations maybe conducted in a competitive manner whereby parties state their positions and negotiate from those positions. It is considered a win/lose strategy or position based strategy. It is the most common form of negotiation strategy that everyone is familiar with, though not the most effective, as it focuses only on the negotiating a party's wants and needs and does not address the needs and wants or desires of the other party. Many people not familiar with negotiating will tend to follow the competitive style approach, which in many situations will not succeed.

33.2.3 Cooperative-Style (Interest-Based) Negotiation

Negotiations may also be conducted as a cooperative process or interest based process whereby the parties focus on solving each other's problems and addressing both parties needs and desires. It is, in other words, a win/win strategy or interest based negotiation strategy.

Parties may use one or the other negotiation strategy of win/lose, or both, or hybrids of both if needed. It is common to use both strategies in one negotiation. Using the strategies depends on how parties perceive negotiations and often whether they want a short-term relationship or long-term relationship with the other party.

In many situations, it is imperative to know the BATNA of the other side. This may facilitate negotiations, as the parties may try to solve each other's problems. Failure to solve your counterpart's main concerns and issues may lead to failed negotiations. Of course, your counterpart has his or her own BATNA. Here is an example of what companies may face when negotiating.

XYZ Company in Korea wants to distribute product XXX in Thailand. Thailand's laws prevent direct sales. XYZ wants to find a distributor that can distribute its product XXX.

Bainai is willing to become a distributor. It costs $1 million in investment and setup costs to distribute product XXX. To recoup its investment, Bainai wants a five-year exclusive contract.

XYZ knows it can find other distributors later, but it needs a distributor now. It does not want to sign an exclusive arrangement with Bainai. What if Bainai is a poor distributor?

Question—What win/win solutions can XYZ and Bainai propose to each other so each can meet its BATNA, or solve each other's interests?

33.2.4 Negotiation Stage

The negotiation stage or middle stage of the negotiation process involves numerous decisions too. Once parties have finalized the pre-negotiation stage, decisions still have to be made involving such issues as when, where, and how negotiations will take place.

For instance, parties may start negotiations via e-mail to negotiate minor items before concluding negotiations over the phone. Or they may start negotiations over the phone and wrap up with face-to-face negotiations. Or they may start with using email to negotiate minor items, phone conferences to settle some other items and then meet face to face to conclude the most important items and issues. Therefore, decisions have to be made on how to negotiate to one's own advantage.

During the negotiation stage, internal and/or external parties and stakeholders may play a part in the outcome. Decisions must be made whether to include them or not. If third parties are involved in negotiations, one or both of the main parties may try to develop coalitions. Third parties may, in fact, add more problems and issues to negotiations or at least bring an added dimension to the discussions.

Parties must also decide upon a venue for negotiations. Many parties prefer a neutral site. However, those negotiators in a strong position may prefer negotiations to be held in their own office. It is all about tactics and to a certain degree perception of the other party's position.

33.2.5 Post-negotiation

An equally important stage is the last stage of negotiations or the post-negotiation stage. This stage results in an agreement or resolution. Hopefully an enforceable one at that.

Parties must also decide whether to reduce an agreement to writing or leave it verbal—or a little bit of both. There are several sub—processes in this stage, such as concluding an agreement, drafting it in writing, and having the parties review it and approve it. Of course, each party may need its home office or upper management to approve the agreement as well.

Parties may want their respective Law Departments or outside lawyers to review the negotiated agreements. Agreements need to be reviewed to determine if they indeed resolve the dispute, and if the agreements are enforceable. A non-enforceable agreement usually does not solve the matter in dispute.

33.3 Miscellaneous Issues

There are a number of miscellaneous issues that parties need to consider when using negotiations as an LRM tool. As negotiations are in fact voluntary, they require the informed consent or assent of the parties. This leads to a number of questions that must be asked.

- Do you resolve the dispute now or wait until a later date? Is now the right time to resolve the dispute?
- Do you use this as an on-going process or see it as an onetime event?
- How many people will participate in the negotiations? Will there be several teams?
- What do you really hope or want to achieve?
- Does the other side want to come to the table?
- What does the other side really want or hope to achieve?
- What is the other side's BATNA? Can you find it out? Can you guess it ?

So both parties must decide if they want to negotiate, and if so, when, where, and how. Maybe delays will benefit one or the other party or maybe not.

It is obvious that negotiation is an important LRM tool. However, to be adequately used as a method to decrease risk of litigation, the parties on both sides (of the negotiation) must be adequately trained in negotiation techniques and must have a proper negotiation mind-set. If the parties come to the table properly prepared, ready to negotiate and seek an amicable outcome, negotiation can be a powerful resolution process and risk mitigation tool. If not, it may lead to a lost opportunity and an unfavorable result.

34

Negotiation: Hypothetical Case in Point

The Glass Works

Fine Glass, a US LCD manufacturer, was approached by Dong A Glass Company out of Korea to create a joint venture in country X. The JV was to be 51 percent owned by Fine Glass with 49 percent owned by Dong A. The purpose behind the JV was the creation of an LCD panel manufacturing facility. Dong A (though in the TV business) did not have access to leading edge LCD panels. Fine Glass was known for its LCD panel-making technology. This facility would be state of the art. It would compete with its major competitors anywhere in the world. The parties discussed the JV to be 75 percent funded by Dong A, with Fine Glass providing all technology and 25 percent of the remaining start-up capital.

Fine Glass was interested because a JV facility would give it access to Asian markets. Besides it would have 51 percent ownership of the JV. What could go wrong?

Fine appointed its VP of international investment, Mr. Brown, to be the point person. He soon realized there would be issues because part of Fine's LCD IP was owned via a joint development agreement by the Japan Glass Company out of Tokyo, Japan. Brown decided to approach Japan Glass about the JV. Japan Glass was interested. After several weeks of phone calls and faxes, Brown met with Mr. Kosigi of Japan Glass in Tokyo to discuss its involvement with the JV. Japan Glass did not want to invest in the JV, but wanted a technical assistance agreement where it could charge the JV a 10 percent royalty. It wouldn't have to worry about repatriation of investment capital.

It was decided the JV was to be headquartered in country X. But for tax purposes and lower manufacturing costs, the parties, including Dong A, soon realized it made more sense to put the physical plant in country Y. X had just completed a tax investment treaty with Y that made investment very attractive. Also, labor costs would be cheaper. Dong A had thought about building an LCD TV factory in Y. Perhaps the JV could be built in the same corporate park where the TV factory would be built.

One problem was that the place where the JV could be built in country Y would be decided by the Y Land Development Corporation, (YLC) a semi-governmental-owned agency assigned the task of approving foreign investment in country Y.

Mr. Brown was dispatched to Seoul to start negotiations with Dong A and Japan Glass. Upon his arrival, he went directly to his hotel. While checking in he suffered a minor heart attack. The meeting was postponed, and Mr. Brown returned to the United States for treatment. Mr. Brown's replacement, Mr. Smith, was tasked with completing the deal. He had no international experience but was next in line for Brown's position.

Smith was under pressure. The delay in meetings because of Brown's heart attack could delay the JV because of the foreign investment process. Also, Smith found out that the country Y land development company was recommending Y own 51 percent of the manufacturing facility in Y, regardless of who owned the JV.

Japan Glass was getting nervous. Its joint development agreement with Fine was legally binding. But if it provided technical assistance to the JV in Y (it would receive a 10 percent royalty), would its IP (patents and trade secrets) be honored by the factory in country Y?

The meeting was set for April 1. Dong A rented out meeting rooms at a major hotel in X, as it did not have adequate office space for meetings. Mr. Park would lead the Dong A team. He spoke English and Korean as well as Japanese. All parties gathered to discuss the creation of the JV, the negotiation of the technical assistance agreement, and the foreign investment application process, etc.

- If you are Mr. Smith, how do you prepare for the negotiations?
- If you are Mr. Park, what cultural differences do you expect to see in the negotiations?
- If you are Mr. Kosigi from Japan Glass, how do you expect to negotiate your issues?
- If you are Mr. Smith, what would you do differently than in a regular domestic transaction?
- In which language would you conduct the negotiations?
- Should an interpreter be used?

35

Use of Arbitration and Dispute Resolution

Form: Arbitration Clauses

35.1 What Is Arbitration?

Arbitration is a contractual mechanism that parties use to avoid litigation. As it is a contractual mechanism, the parties are free to determine the procedural requirements, number of arbitrators, governing law, and other key provisions, etc.

In other words, arbitration is a procedure that the parties select instead of availing themselves of a judicial system of a particular country, state, or province.

The primary characteristics of arbitration are:

- The parties select the arbitrator(s).
- It is a consensual process.
- It is a private process.
- It is a neutral process.
- It issues a final decision, with normally no appeal rights.
- It is very cost effective.

35.2 Justification for Arbitration

The main reasons that make arbitration a very attractive process over litigation, especially in the United States, are primarily: (1) it is a neutral process, (2) arbitral decisions are easily enforceable, (3) it offers flexibility (the ability to control and minimize electronic discovery and cost), and (4) the arbitrations are sophisticated. Flexibility, sophistication of the arbitral process, and enforceability are set forth in more detail below.

- Flexibility: One of the most fascinating qualities of arbitration, both domestic and international, is its inherent flexibility. That quality principally arises from two sources: the fact that the contract of the parties creates the jurisdiction of the arbitrator, and the necessity to adapt to the procedural requirements of the claimants and respondents. Examples of flexibility include provisions for the type of arbitrator required, and rules regarding the admission of evidence and discovery of facts. That is particularly important for any company that engages in business in the United States due to the explosion of discovery requirements regarding electronic documents. US courts impose stringent requirements for the maintenance of electronic documents (such as e-mails) and enforce severe penalties for violating these rules. These rules are particularly onerous on companies that have documents stored in various countries and locations. The arbitration clause negotiated can protect a party from such requirements while still maintaining due process and the ability to prove one's case.
- Sophistication of arbitrators/process: Although arbitrators usually have legal training, they come from many different backgrounds—law professors, practicing lawyers, judges, government officials, etc. This fact creates an opportunity for the development of a sophistication that flows from the combing of many different experiences and points of

view. Moreover, because all arbitral tribunals are ad hoc in the sense that they are created for a specific case and cease to exist when that matter is determined, an experienced arbitrator encounters numerous significant collegial experiences on a level and variety that is not available to the judge. This leads to a willingness to devise solutions to procedural and substantive matters that are sophisticated in the sense that they are worldly wise and are prepared to accept complexity. For example, if a dispute is of a technical nature, the parties can require that the arbitrator be experienced in specific fields (e.g., engineering, employment law, or commercial actions of a particular type). This leads to sophisticated techniques of questioning expert witnesses, as well as other obvious benefits.

- Enforceability: It is a truism that an award issued by an arbitral tribunal and a judgment rendered by a court are worth very little unless it can be enforced. Happily, arbitral awards are easily enforced. Sometimes, in certain circumstances, they are more easily enforced than court-rendered judgments. In the United States, the enforcement of arbitral awards is guaranteed by the Federal Arbitration Act and numerous state laws. Indeed, if an international dispute exists between parties of different countries, the New York Convention (signed by the United States and most other nations) makes enforcement of arbitral awards easier than court-rendered judgments by virtue of limiting the defenses that may be interposed to enforcement of the arbitral award.

- Arbitration has long been viewed favorably as a dispute resolution mechanism for international disputes. This especially holds true for disputes in Asia.[1] In the past

---

[1] Bryan Hopkins, "A Comparison of Recent Changes in the Arbitral Laws and Regulations of Hong Kong, Singapore and Korea," *KLRI Journal of Law and Legislation* 3, no. 1 (2013).

decade, arbitration in Asia has greatly increased which is an outcome or result of the rapid increase in trade.[2]

35.3 Arbitration Process: General Characteristics

General Characteristics: The arbitral process begins with the arbitration clause. When drafting an arbitration provision, several options are available. For example, an arbitration clause can include a provision first requiring mediation prior to proceeding with an arbitration. Thus, under this scenario a party can go to mediation, and if there is an agreement, the process ends there. If not, then the parties proceed to arbitration and a final award. The arbitration clause must also deal with the place of arbitration, the language of arbitration, and the type of arbitrators to be selected. The place of arbitration can be important, particularly in international disputes, because the law of the venue of the arbitration will be applicable on procedural matters where there is a dispute among the parties.

Arbitration clause: The first step in the arbitral procedure is the drafting of the arbitration clause. The following are the essentials of any arbitration clause:

- Include a mediation requirement if desired (strict time limits should be imposed and an administrative body selected to manage the mediation).
- A broad description of what is covered (e.g., "and dispute that arises from or is related to" a particular contract). This is important to make sure that the obligation to arbitrate is not avoided by a party arguing that a particular dispute is not covered by the arbitration provision.
- An institution to administer the arbitration (e.g., the International Chamber of Commerce (ICC), the American Arbitration Association (AAA), the London Court of

---

[2] Ibid

International Arbitration (LCIA), etc. This is important to ensure that the process is not unduly delayed.

- Place of arbitration (make sure that the laws of the venue are arbitration friendly and provide for finality of the award).
- Arbitration award must be final.
- Number, process of selection, and qualifications of arbitrators.
- Law applicable to the dispute.
- Discovery concerns (how many depositions, limitations on e-discovery, etc.).
- Ability to obtain provisional remedies (e.g., injunctive relief) from courts without waiving rights to arbitration.
- Confidentiality.

35.3.1 Arbitral Procedure

Upon a dispute arising that is covered by an arbitration clause, the procedure regarding filing a demand or request for arbitration is simple. First and foremost, the rules of the administrative body selected to run the mediation must be consulted. However, the (very) general procedural steps are as follows:

- In the event mediation is called for in the arbitration clause, initiate mediation with a recognized mediation body. Several administrative bodies, such as the ICC (International Chamber of Commerce) and AAA (American Arbitration Association), provide for mediation rules as well. Typically a demand for mediation with a statement of the dispute and a filing fee are filed. The opposing party will then be entitled to file its own statement. The parties attempt to agree on a mediator; if not, the administrative body will select the mediator. The mediation is to be governed by strict time limits, at the conclusion of which the arbitration process can begin.

- A demand/request for arbitration is filed with the appropriate arbitral body, accompanied by a filing fee. What is included in the demand/request for arbitration is determined by the applicable rules and judgment of counsel at the time of filing. Typically the respondent will have to file its answer and will be responsible for half the costs of the arbitration. (Consumer arbitration differs significantly in this regard.)
- Arbitrators are selected, and the arbitration process begins. The production of documents and other evidence begins as circumscribed by the arbitral clause. In many circumstances, direct testimony will be provided in written form, and only cross-examination and limited redirect is allowed at the final hearings. Prehearing memorials are typically filed. A final hearing is held, after which the arbitral tribunal will issue a final award.
- Upon the issuance of a final award, if the losing party does not voluntarily comply with the award, then the award is presented to a court of competent jurisdiction, where it is confirmed and will be enforced as any other court judgment.

35.4 Arbitral Institutions

A number of arbitral institutions have become popular, especially in the international context. Many countries have their own arbitration laws as well as arbitral bodies that administer arbitration. The most popular are:

- The International Chamber of Commerce (ICC)
- The American Arbitration Association (AAA)
- The International Center of Dispute Resolution (ICDR)

Many companies that do business in Asia use the arbitration rules of Singapore (SIAC); Hong Kong (HKIAC) or Seoul (KCAB). To date, more arbitrations are beginning to take place in mainland

China, as well. The increase of arbitrations in the Asia –Pacific countries are directly related to the increase in trade and rapid economic growth of the Asia region. This is expected to continue.

35.5 Arbitration Clause

The arbitration clause is the most important part of any contract when the parties are negotiating the use of arbitration.

A well-thought-out arbitration clause should contain:

- If possible, a mediation requirement—to possibly avoid arbitration
- A broad description of what is covered
- An institution to administer arbitration (ICC, AAA, ICDR, etc.)
- Place of arbitration (the laws of the venue should be arbitration friendly)
- An understanding that arbitration awards are final
- Number, process of selection, and qualification of arbitrators
- Applicable law
- Discovery concerns (limitations to E-discovery and use of ESI)

In light of the current climate, no one wants to incur costs associated with arbitration of litigation if avoidable. To help avoid arbitration or potential excessive costs, I recommend the following:

- The arbitration clause should also require a period of time (thirty days, etc.) where the dispute is first escalated to executive management to discuss. You will be surprised how easy it is to settle a dispute when the senior-level management, who understand the "big picture," gets involved.
- As stated before, try to make use of mediation as well. Having a neutral party look at a claim and provide an objective opinion on the claim could lead to a speedy resolution.

- Make certain the arbitration rules and administrative body fit the scope of the deal. How expensive is the deal?
- Limit the scope and length of arbitration as well as the discovery permitted. Limitations on discovery can help not only speed up arbitration but limit and control costs.
- Think about negotiating a prevailing party cost/recovery expense provision in the clause. This would certainly cause the parties to think more about settlement of a dispute instead of arbitration.
- In-house counsel must manage and control arbitration costs. Outside counsel needs to understand the need to control costs and should agree to an arbitration budget. A well-thought-out arbitration budget is very important. The costs of arbitration will depend on how well in-house and arbitration counsel manage the process.

36

Arbitration: Hypothetical Case in Point

Mining Coal

Xxx Construction had just finished a profitable year. It had completed the luxury skyscraper in Mumbai and had also finished building a new SBR plant in Saudi Arabia. However, due to a shortage of steel from its supplier of steel, The Steel Company, it was limited in future projects. So, Mr. Shin, president of XXX Construction, decided to go into the steel business.

XXX obtained bank financing from its bank, Acme Bank, for $100 million to buy an old steel mill owned by YYY Steel. Terms of financing included a guaranteed repayment of $10 million to Acme upon the completion of the first construction project using steel from the YYY facility.

One problem that XXX had was, of course, lack of natural resources. To make steel, XXX needed iron ore and coal for the furnaces. XXX was able to source one hundred thousand tons of iron ore per year from Kazakhstan. However, XXX could not source coal as well.

Luckily, President Shin's GM, Mr. Lee, called. He had a source in China that should be able to provide coal. Mr. Lee contacted the Homin Mining Company and was able to negotiate a supply contract for two hundred thousand tons of coal per year. According to the contract between XXX Construction and Homin, the coal would be delivered to XXX's carrier (a ship) at the port of Hunan every Friday starting sixty days from execution of the contract. The supply contract was signed on March 1, 2010. President Shin was very happy, as a worldwide shortage in coal was expected in 2011, and he had firmed up a source of supply.

Knowing that he had iron ore and coal, Shin set about executing construction agreements, which would use the steel made by the newly acquired YYY Steel plant. One of the contracts was with the Premium Office Tower Company for the construction of a modern luxury office /hotel building in downtown New York City. The steel was to be delivered to the construction site in NYC on July 1, 2012. Because of the construction permits, unions, and tax benefits provided by NYC, construction had to be commenced no later than June 1 and finished on June 1, 2013. Failure to complete construction on time would result in holdback penalties of $100,000 per week to be levied against XXX. Shin was confident the schedule could be met. What could go wrong?

On May 1, 2012, Mr. Shin received a frantic call from Mr. Lee. The coal from China was not delivered. In fact, it may not be delivered for at least another eight months due to logistical problems. Homin Mining did not realize the train from its mine could not deliver the coal to the port of Hunan because train tracks had not been laid all the way to the port. The tracks stopped twenty miles from the port. The port of Hunan was responsible for the track. No construction of new tracks was scheduled until 2013. To make matters worse, there were no roads on which to have the train offload onto trucks.

Among the problems:

- Due to a worldwide shortage of coal, YYY Steel could not produce any steel for at least four months. It found a new source of coal in Brazil, but it would take three months to have it delivered. The coal was selling for $150 per metric ton instead of $100 per metric ton from China.

- The ship sent to pick up the coal in China was being charged demurrage charges of $10,000 per day for every day it stayed at the port of Hunan.
- The construction schedule of the new office building in NYC was threatened.
- If XXX could not perform on schedule, it would have to pay a penalty and still had to think about repaying part of the loan to Citibank.

XXX faced massive losses. Its steel mill, YYY Steel, was in trouble. Also, it faced penalties and fines if it could not complete the construction of the office building in NYC on time. It was four months behind schedule. Its carrier also faced demurrage charges as well.

Mr. Shin called up his lawyer, Mr. Smith. Mr. Smith had reviewed the supply contract with Tsintao and the construction agreement with Premium. Mr. Shin wanted to know what kind of dispute he was looking at and what his options were. Both agreements contained an arbitration clause. The supply contract's arbitration clause stated in part:

All disputes arising out of or in connection with the present contract shall be submitted to the International Court of Arbitration of the International Chamber of Commerce and shall be finally settled under the rules of arbitration of the International Chamber of Commerce by arbitrators appointed in accordance with said rules.

Upon reflection, Mr. Smith realized the supply agreement was silent as to where the arbitration was to take place, number of arbitrators, and governing law.

- If XXX is forced to arbitrate its claim against Homin for damages, what concerns does it have?

- Should XXX expect three arbitrators or one arbitrator?
- What language will the arbitration be in?
- Where will the arbitration take place?
- What issues does Homin face?
- What advantages are there to arbitration over litigation?

37

Management of Litigation

Form: Litigation Plan and Budget

Management of litigation, like management of most business processes, begins with a business plan and a budget. In this case, prior to trial, when a company seeks an appropriate law firm to represent it, it needs an acceptable litigation plan and budget. Law firms many times will try to push back on the request of a budget, claiming legal costs are hard to predict. This, of course, is not the case. Experienced lawyers, whether in the United States, Europe, or Asia, are very familiar with the legal costs in their own geographic region as well as costs and expenses associated with the particular issue, such as patent litigation or class actions. Certain costs may be hard to quantify, such as defense litigation costs (which may depend on how aggressive a plaintiff is in trial), but for the most part, law firms can provide a litigation plan and budget using approximate or ballpark figures.

Effective management of litigation will depend on a well-prepared litigation plan and budget. This, in turn, depends on the proper identification of potential litigation issues and a plan for potentially adversarial proceedings. Questions that should be asked when discussing the plan and budget with outside counsel include:

- Is this matter an actual or potentially adversarial proceeding?
- Will this matter result in potential commercial litigation?
- Will this matter result in potential regulatory litigation?
- Will this matter lead to governmental litigation?

37.1 Kinds of Actions

An accurate litigation plan and budget will depend on the nature of the proceeding or legal matter at hand. Such matters can be classified as follows:

- Commercial litigation
- Antitrust and trade disputes
- Bankruptcy and creditor actions
- Class actions (product liability, etc.)
- Labor and employment
- Regulatory proceedings
- Governmental inquiry/informal visit
- Investigations
- Subpoenas
- Government enforcement proceedings
- Administrative tribunals
- Internal corporate investigations

Certain costs will be associated with the nature of the dispute. For instance, commercial litigation costs will be dictated by the cost of discovery, including: depositions, interrogatories, production of documents and things, and physical examinations, etc. Costs involved with regulatory proceedings will involve governmental investigations and internal corporate investigations and perhaps parallel proceedings, criminal as well as civil litigation.

37.2 Litigation Management Tools

Litigation management depends upon the in-house legal team or risk manager actively assessing and managing litigation by using an effective litigation management process. The litigation management process should utilize management processes as well as LRM tools.

For a corporation to effectively manage litigation, management needs to understand its role as litigation manager. If it hands over the entire litigation management process to the outside firm representing it, the costs will, of course, substantially increase! The law firm must be managed! The risk manager, corporate manager, or in-house lawyer (General Counsel, etc.) must understand his or her role as a litigation manager. That includes use of management functions and LRM tools.

- Management functions
  - Effective coordination of legal defense efforts to avoid duplication of costs
  - Coordination of use of witness and discovery
  - Serve as the central site for all facts, positions, and decisions in legal issues
  - Development and implementation of a defense plan
  - Internal assessment of facts
  - Point of contact for regulators
- LRM tools
- Litigation budget
- Coordination of documents
- Use of employee interviews
- Insurance
- Use of defense plan
- Early case assessment
- Alternative fees
- Outside billing guidelines

38

Litigation Management during Trial

Effective litigation management during trial depends on the company's attitude toward litigation as well as its controls over the law firm. Trials, especially in the United States are quite expensive and could involve the future existence of the companies involved.

Trials by their very nature are very costly. Normally, lawsuits settle prior to trial, as both sides know that juries can be fickle. Some companies will, therefore, never want to go to trial (or try to settle during trial), and some will decide to fight and go to trial. Many times it is more advantageous for parties to litigation to settle prior to trial, as trials become extremely expensive.

Disadvantages of trials include:

- High transaction costs
- Length of proceedings
- Negative publicity
- Business interruption
- Unpredictability of juries
- Lack of finality—always the loser will appeal

If a company decides to go to trial, it must control the outside law firm, manage the process, and understand the potential dangers (including cost and expenses) it faces. Prior to trial, the company needs to ask trial counsel a number of questions, including:

- What is the true evaluation of the case?
- What is the approximate cost of trial?
- What are the chances of settlement before trial?
- What are the main strategies of litigating the case?
- What witnesses and experts will be needed?
- How long will the trial last?
- What are the chances of winning?

If a company knows it only has a 30 to 40 percent chance of winning at trial, is the dispute worth going to trial for, or is settlement a better option? A company is in a better position to decide whether it should go to trial upon proper evaluation of the case. LRM tools can help this.

38.1 Evaluation of the Case

At the beginning of litigation and selection of the law firm, the risk manager or in-house lawyer must assess the case—the strengths, weaknesses, costs, etc., involved. Case evaluation is very important. Evaluation can be made through an early evaluation by outside counsel, knowledge of potential costs, use of employee interviews, and formulation of a plan/budget. When a company has a good idea on the chances of winning, potential costs, and weaknesses of the case, it is in a better position to determine whether to proceed to trial. Therefore, at the beginning of litigation, the company or organization should obtain a thorough evaluation of the case and use internal tools to assess the cost of a trial. Is the cost of litigation worth it?

Risk analysis of litigation can be a useful tool in evaluating a case. One such tool that is often utilized is the decision tree. A decision tree analysis can be used to evaluate the probability of outcome of certain events during trial. Each event can then be analyzed in the context of the probability of the entire outcome. As Carol Basri and Irving Kagan point out, a decision tree risk analysis allows "a rigorous and systematic method of analyzing and preparing cases from inception."[1]

38.2 Fees during Litigation

Obviously, the litigation budget should address the fees and costs of going to trial; a law firm's fees at trial skyrocket for a number of reasons, including:

- The number of lawyers involved.
- Time: Most trial lawyers will work long hours during a trial, so fees will add up. This is especially true if the trial is a complex one involving patent disputes or antitrust claims.
- The cost of expert witnesses.
- The cost of motions during trial. Motion practice can be very expensive.
- The cost of producing documents during trial.
- Note: If you are spending $100,000 per month before trial, you may spend $500,000 during trial, especially if it lasts longer than you or your outside counsel originally thought.

38.3 Evaluation of Discovery Costs during Trial

Discovery costs in litigation are usually the largest part of the total cost of litigation. Discovery costs (in the United States) can add up to 50 percent or more of the total cost of litigation. Depending on the trial, discovery costs can increase, especially if there are spoliation issues or document destruction issues. Corporations must constantly monitor discovery issues during

---

[1] Carole Basri and Irving Kagan, *Corporate Legal Departments*, Third Edition (New York: Practising Law Institute, 2004), 14–24.

litigation to prevent surprises. A spoliation motion at trial could be very costly, consuming time and expense not originally anticipated. Don't just rely on outside counsel to handle all discovery issues.

38.4 To Settle or Not Settle?

There will come a time during litigation, especially at trial, where it may be advantageous to settle the case instead of continuing with the trial or going to the verdict phase of the trial. Some companies will want to settle early in the process and some later. It depends on the strategy of the company and how it views its chances of winning. It also depends on advice of the trial counsel the company has hired, as well as other factors, such as pressure from the judge, lack of confidence in the jury (do they appear to dislike you or your lawyer?), and overtures from the other side. More importantly, it depends on what is in the best interests of the company. Outside counsel will not necessarily think about the best interests of the company. The law firm, or your trial counsel, will want to win! That's expected. That what they want to do! In fact, you probably retained the outside law firm to win. But winning may not be in the company's best interests. Settling a case prior to trial may not only save the company money, time and expense but may also prevent negative publicity thereby saving the company's brand. Do not get so caught up in the emotion of litigation that you forget to settle when it is to your advantage.

38.5 Evaluation of the Trial

Effective management of litigation during the trial process requires an up-to-date evaluation of the trial. This requires close contact with the outside counsel handling the trial, observing the trial (how does your trial counsel look at the trial?), constant feedback from your litigation lawyer or team, and involvement of management. The litigation manager of a company needs not only to stay involved throughout the trial but must update management on a daily basis.

A risk manager, litigation manager, or in-house counsel must manage the litigation process, especially during trial. It is important that the risk manager or in-house counsel stay connected with the trial counsel and consider doing the following action items during trial:

- Get a summary of the trial from your trial counsel or his team on a regular basis, preferable every day. Are there are any surprises in how the case is proceeding? If so what are they?
- Monitor the jury. If a jury is deciding the case, how does the jury look? Do you think the jury is interested in the case and your side of the argument?
- Determine if the defense strategies used in trial are working. If not, is it time to settle?
- Determine if settlement is the best option. Use the decision tree analysis to help make Alternative Dispute Resolution (ADR) decisions.
- Trials can be very expensive. Success depends on a number of factors including the following:
  - Facts of the case.
  - Trial strategy. Is it working?
  - Correct evaluation of the case prior to trial.
  - Correct evaluation of the case during trial.
  - Attitude of the judge towards your case
  - The makeup of the jury.

Successful management of litigation during the trial depends on use of LRM tools such as case evaluation, coordination of witnesses, and trial strategy. If a company fails to properly manage litigation during the trial phase, it can lead to increased costs, expenses, business interruption, and, of course, defeat. Therefore, use of litigation management tools such as a decision tree analysis, document coordination system, or early case assessment process is very important.

SUMMARY

L RM processes are numerous and diverse. Such processes can touch upon all departments of a company. The problem in-house counsel or risk management face is that it is not without cost. In order to properly implement an LRM program, executive management has to understand it and approve its implementation.

In other words, in-house counsel or risk management must sell it to the BOD. This can be done with empirical data showing historical legal costs, insurance costs and probable legal fees based on potential legal exposure.

PART 5

Legal Risk Management: Evaluation of the Process

39

Legal Risk Management: Evaluation of the Process

39.1 Selling Legal Risk Management to the Organization

A discussion of legal risk management (LRM) in the proceeding chapters has illuminated the numerous processes and procedures that should be applied. LRM processes are not only numerous and diverse, but can, if accepted and implemented by the organization, provide an effective way of mitigating and/or eliminating legal exposure and prevent claims, litigation, and fines. The problem for any corporate risk manager or in-house counsel is to sell the LRM process to management. It is not without cost and expense.

Most organizations have yet to fully embrace, implement, and internalize risk management concepts, let alone LRM processes. Studies have shown corporations have yet to fully embrace risk management concepts and have failed to implement an enterprise wide risk monitoring and reporting system. How do you sell LRM to the organization? First you need to quantify the legal risk and exposure to enable the CFO and other executives and perhaps board members to understand the significance of the exposure the organization faces.

39.2 Quantify the Legal Exposure

Quantifying potential legal exposure is fairly easy. One can look at historical legal costs, expenses, and related jury verdicts, fines, etc., to determine a base line for future legal costs and expenses. If an historical record of legal costs does not exist, numerous reports and surveys exist on how to average legal costs and expenses via a particular industry. Your insurance broker may have summaries of legal costs for your industry. At least it should have a historical summary of insurance related claims. Once one has enough empirical data to show potential exposure, it is easy to show potential legal costs. In fact, a number of companies in the legal industry have issues benchmarking reports breaking down the average legal costs and expenses in particular industries. This can be a great tool to use when showing management what costs and expenses are normally incurred by companies.

The CFO of any organization is numbers driven. If you can provide, in effect, "the bottom line" to the CFO, he will be inclined to approve a budget for LRM processes. Be prepared and have facts and figures to support your request.

39.3 A "Teaching Moment"

Do not be afraid to use crises, disasters, lawsuits, government investigations and fines, etc., to your advantage. Companies, especially large companies, tend to throw resources at perceived problems and exposure once a crisis happens. A crisis may be an event that will justify legal spending.

Use such an unfortunate event or crisis to not only explain why the LRM program is needed, but use it as a "teaching moment" of what not to do. Take advantage of it! Remember, sometimes organizations move slowly until they perceive a threat of financial loss or exposure. Then, once the company perceives a threat they throw money and resources as it.

If the CEO, CFO, etc., turns on the TV and sees your company's product shown in a negative light, that is a good time to request a budget for risk management or an LRM program. Teaching moments are often good tools to use as well.

40

Internalization of Legal Risk Management

Most companies have yet to internalize legal risk management. Though many companies have some LRM processes in place, those normally are few and far between. Also, though organizations may have a few processes in place, they are usually not coordinated with each other internally. Sometimes departments do not communicate with each other as effectively as they should.

To be completely effective, a company has to internalize LRM processes. What does this call for? Basically, a company internalizes the LRM process when:

- LRM is embedded in the corporate decision-making process.
- The identification of early warning indicators are based on key LRM processes.
- Effective use of LRM tools on a regular and /or daily basis.

A company internalizes the LRM process when it not only fully implements the LRM process and uses tools to identify all major areas of legal risk but also uses it in the decision-making process.

Only when a company is willing to fully embrace legal risk management can it reap the benefits of preventing, mitigating, controlling, and transferring legal risk.

41

Review of Legal Risk Management: Justification

At the beginning of the book, we discussed the concept of LRM, why it is important and why organizations need to adopt it. As you can see from the many areas covered in this book, from risk insurance to compliance and law firm management, LRM is not only a broad area, but it consists of many diverse processes and tools. A company cannot emphasize only one aspect of LRM and forget the rest. After all, the goal of LRM is to prevent, manage, mitigate, and transfer legal risk, allowing a company to control its own future. Taking a proactive stand with regard to risk allows a company to control its destiny instead of reacting to events!

These days, companies are exposed to unprecedented attacks from many sources. Governments want to increase taxation and regulation; the media wants to attack companies, and, of course, people are accustomed to looking at companies as the "root of all evil." To defend itself against attack from many sources, a company has to implement as well as internalize a culture of "legal risk management." A well designed, implemented, and internalized LRM program can control legal risk, allowing a company or organization to prosper.

It is hoped that this book has, in some small way, contributed to the understanding of risk management from the legal perspective.

66

Hopefully, it arms a risk manager or in-house counsel with enough ammunition to not only justify an LRM program to upper management of an organization but to obtain adequate resources to implement it. Good luck!

SUMMARY

Though a company should be proactive and implement LRM processes before litigation happens, it can still mitigate costs and expenses by implementing processes during or in anticipation of litigation. This involves litigation management's use of corporate structures to transfer risk and manage outside counsel.

Companies can transfer legal risk or mitigate legal exposure through the appropriate use of the corporate structure. For multinationals or those organizations with subsidiaries, the use of a holding company can help insulate a company by isolating liability to individual subsidiaries. Obviously, however, drawbacks have to be considered, including costs and having to use proper corporate formalities.

Once a company realizes it will face litigation, the most important LRM processes it will have to use are those involving litigation management. In other words, what processes are in place to pick a law firm, manage the law firm, and control legal costs and expenses? Only with a robust LRM process that requires a company to properly manage outside counsel can the company avoid lengthy litigation and the resulting excessive fees and costs.

A number of tools can be used to manage litigation. Standard LRM tools include the use of a litigation budget, use of a defense plan, outside counsel billing guidelines, and early case assessment.

CONCLUSION

Legal risk management (LRM) is very similar to the concept of ERM, or enterprise risk management. ERM is the management of risk across a corporation; LRM is the management of legal and corporate risk across a corporation. As such, it impacts all divisions and departments and requires constant implementation and the support of executive management. Only with the support of management can LRM become truly imbedded in the decision-making process of the organization.

In-house counsel and risk managers alike, whether in the Compliance Division or Insurance Department, need to take ownership of this important and vital concept. A company without a LRM process operates at risk and faces great exposure.

It is hoped that this book, in some small way, contributes to the understanding of risk management from the legal perspective. Hopefully it arms a risk manager or in-house counsel with enough ammunition to not only justify an LRM program to upper management of an organization but to obtain adequate resources to implement it.

ABOUT THE AUTHOR

Bryan E. Hopkins
Sejong University

Bryan Hopkins is professor of law at Sejong University in Seoul, Korea. He received his Juris Doctor from Florida State University in 1980. From 1999 to 2010 he was VP and General Counsel of Samsung Electronics America. Prior to working at Samsung Electronics America, he was Counsel at Racal Electronics and Assistant General Counsel at Kumho Petrochemical in Seoul, Korea. He has published articles in the *Asia-Mensa Counsel* magazine, as well as the *KLRI Journal of Law and Legislation* in Korea. He has extensive experience in compliance, e-discovery, litigation management, and risk management.

APPENDIX A

Loss Control
Policy and Procedure Manual

- Policy Statement

It is, and shall continue to be, a primary objective of each of its divisions and subsidiaries to provide customers with safe and reliable products and services. Our employees must be committed to fulfilling these needs. Each operating division is responsible for maintaining effective control of the conditions necessary to meet the safety needs of our customers and control product claim losses.

- Program Objective

To increase the awareness and effectiveness of product loss control and claims defense programming through the development and application of effective procedures and controls.

- Organization: Responsibility

Company vice presidents and officers are responsible for the development, application, and maintenance of Products Loss Control – Claim Defense Programs, consistent with the guidelines of this policy, at each of their respective operating locations.

In turn, the administration application and maintenance of such programs on a current and continuous basis rests with the individual company/division chief operating officers.

Depending upon circumstances, a company/division chief operating officer may appoint a representative to coordinate activities on his or her behalf.

All policy statements, Products Loss Control Programs, and related formal announcements and directives concerning individual programs should be approved and signed by the respective company/division chief operating officer. (See sample Policy Statement – exhibit A attached.)

Will issue general policies and procedures, monitor activity, and provide coordinating assistance with the broker and insurance company.

- Products Loss Control – Claim Defense Committee

Each division/subsidiary should, either independently or in conjunction with related group members, establish a Products Loss Control – Claim Defense Committee. The company/division officer, or where applicable their appointed representative, should chair the Committee.

Committee membership will vary depending on the type of operation (manufacturing, service, etc.) and the size of the operation. Each Committee should include the company/division representative (chairperson), the loss control representative, and sufficient membership to provide representation from all strategic departments (i.e., R&D, engineering, design, QA, QC, manufacturing, marketing, service, purchasing, shipping and receiving).

It is anticipated that most committees will have a membership of from three to seven. The minimum is two active members.

Joint committees formed within a related group shall consist of a minimum of one member representative from each involved operating location. Under these conditions, each of the company/division representatives must serve to coordinate the program directly with all affected departments and personnel within their operation. Joint committees should also include representatives of all strategic departments.

The purpose of the Products Loss Control – Claim Defense Committee is to:

- Develop a formal written program
- Implement the program through education and training.
- Provide administrative surveillance and technical product safety assistance and guidance throughout the operation.
- Monitor claims activity.
- Identify real or potential problem areas and institute corrective activity.

[Note: ADD MORE ITEMS HERE IF NEEDED]

Committee meetings should be scheduled and conducted on a regular basis. It is anticipated that, depending upon need, meetings will be scheduled either monthly, semi-monthly, quarterly, or semi-annually. Each operation should, at a minimum, conduct semiannual meetings to review their program. All operations should prepare complete minutes of all meetings and forward copies to the Director of Litigation and Risk Management.

- Research—Design—Development

Research, design, and development of products and services should include both safety and reliability considerations.

Personnel assigned to these activities should possess necessary academic and experience qualifications and meet applicable registration or certification requirements.

Formal hazard/failure evaluations should be conducted on all new products and services. Every possible hazard/failure that could result from use, misuse, or modification should be identified and eliminated whenever possible. Identified danger that cannot be designed out should be identified and given individual attention in the form of special warnings and instructions.

Design efforts should be directed toward meeting or exceeding all applicable safety standards and regulations. These may include federal, state, and local codes and regulation, industry and trade standards, technical society standards, and others that may be applicable to a given product or service.

Laboratory and field tests should be conducted to verify product and service safety and reliability. Where required (or desirable), independent laboratory testing and/or certification should be utilized. Product and service certification by industry or trade associations should also be considered.

All tests, evaluations, findings, and decisions relating to the above should be documented and retained.

Modification of design of existing products and revision of service procedures should include the same considerations.

Procedures should be developed for regular review of established product and service lines to ensure that they continue to meet subsequent safety and reliability standards and regulations.

- Quality Control—Standards and Procedures

Written quality control standards, including specifications, should be developed for all components, materials, and processes critical to product and service safety and reliability. Material specifications should comply with national and/or company standards and meet the requirements of all applicable safety standards.

All purchases should include specifications, regulatory standards, and all other company acceptance criteria that must be adhered to by the supplier. Incoming materials and components should be checked to ensure that they meet minimum standards. Purchase orders should contain provisions for warranties as to the fitness of the products and/or services, compliance with applicable standards, and indemnity agreements to either eliminate or transfer the risk.

Formal procedures for process controls and quality checks should be established. The standards and procedures should be made available for control use in the form of a quality control manual. Educational and training programs should be established as necessary to ensure effective performance.

Quality checks and final tests should be conducted as often as necessary to ensure that applicable standards and specifications are met. Employees conducting checks and tests must possess the necessary skills to certify acceptance. All equipment and tools used for quality control should meet current requirements for product safety and reliability and be maintained in proper operating condition.

Quality checks and final test date relating to the safety and reliability characteristics of products and services should be recorded and maintained so that, within the bounds of good practice, the condition of the products or service can be verified.

As necessary and feasible, parts, materials, units, packages, tools, and equipment crucial to safety should be permanently identified.

- Certificate of Insurance—Vendors Endorsement—Hold Harmless (Indemnification) Agreements

Selection of subcontractors and suppliers should include consideration of their financial responsibility for liability losses.

A certificate of insurance should be obtained from every subcontractor. Certificates should include specific coverages (i.e., products, completed operations, automobile, contractual coverages, etc.) and certify amounts of liability of not less than limits currently carried by.

An individual analysis of the extent of potential liability should be conducted whenever a subcontractor's coverage is less than that of the Company. When the loss liability potential is greater than the amount of coverage, the subcontractor should be requested to increase coverage, or other subcontractors with satisfactory insurance coverage should be solicited.

A determination of a vendor's insurance coverage should be made prior to the purchase of products for eventual resale. If it is determined that sufficient coverage exists to provide acceptable insurance protection for the risk involved, a vendor endorsement should be requested and obtained before actual resale of any items. If sufficient insurance is not available, the vendor should be requested to supply adequate coverage, or other vendors with satisfactory insurance coverage should be solicited.

In many instances the Company and its subsidiaries are required to enter into contracts containing some form of hold harmless (indemnification) agreement. Although there are many types of hold harmless agreements, they generally fall into three broad categories.

- Limited forms hold the other contracting party harmless for claims arising out of your negligence.
- Intermediate forms hold the other party to the contract harmless against claims where both of you may be jointly negligent.
- Broad forms indemnify the other party to the contract even where he is solely responsible (negligent) for the loss.

[NOTE: ADD MORE INSURANCE PROCESSES HERE IF NEEDED]

- Manuals, Instructions, and Labels

Operator's instruction manuals should be developed for all equipment. They should provide instruction for safe use, storage, operation, and maintenance.

The manual should identify the standards of performance in respect to safety that the product should achieve after proper preparation.

Operating instructions should be complete and easily understandable. They should contain special instruction in the use of safety devices and protective equipment. All associated hazards should be clearly identified. The operating instructions should detail the procedures that will protect against these hazards, in direct and understandable language and, as necessary, in illustrations.

Operating instructions should include maintenance instructions, and parts lists servicing instructions should clearly specify the steps necessary to assemble, install, use, and maintain the product in a safe and reliable condition. Special attention should be given to the care of safety devices. All service work performed by the company should be fully documented and retained.

Warnings and caution statements should be included in the manual and on the products and/or the product container in the form of labels or tags. They should, for example, contain statements that:

- Highlight correct methods for assembly, installation, use, and maintenance, and indicate the level of skill or training needed.
- Stress the dangers of not following the printed procedures and instructions.
- Describe the product's limitations.
- Warn against modification of the product and parts substitution.
- Warn of misuse and hazard to the user.
- Specify maintenance procedures and frequency.
- Project the useful life of the product.
- Instruct the user in the care and use of safety devices and protective equipment and warn of potential consequences.
- Recommend antidotes or emergency procedures when applicable.

Labels and warnings must comply with federal, state, local, and industry regulations and standards. The copy should be clear, conspicuous, and complete. Special attention should be given to the physical durability of the materials used for labeling and warning.

Manuals and labels should be reviewed regularly to ensure compliance with regulations and standards. They should be maintained current to warn users of new dangers discovered. Previous purchasers should be warned by the best means available when future developments make a change necessary for safety purposes.

All manuals and labels should be reviewed and approved by the Product Loss Control Committee and legal counsel before actual use.

- Marketing—Sales and Advertising

Sales and advertising materials should accurately describe products and services. Literature and exhibits used in sales promotion, advertising, or public relations should judiciously reflect necessary accident prevention features, such as safe operating practices, proper projective devices, and approved guarding.

Sales, distributor, dealer, installation, and service personnel should accurately picture products and services. They should be included in educational activities concerned with product safety responsibilities. Sales and other technical representatives should not be misrepresented as being more expert than they, in fact, are.

All proposed advertising literature should be reviewed for technical accuracy and exaggerated statements. Terms such as "maintenance free," "absolutely safe," "foolproof," and "nontoxic" should be avoided. All sales and advertising materials should be reviewed on a regular basis.

Disclaimers and limitations of warranties should be incorporated into sales literature and sales agreements whenever possible.

All advertising should be reviewed and approved by the Product Loss Control Committee and legal counsel before distribution.

- Packaging and Shipping

Written standards should be developed for the packaging and shipping of products. Applicable federal and state standards and regulations governing the identification, packaging, and shipment of regulated products must be included. Company safe packaging and shipping standards should be developed for all products.

Formal procedures should be developed to ensure completeness of shipments, including compliance with shipping and safety standards. Special attention should be directed toward ensuring that all information and instruction manuals, labels, warnings, and safety devices are included in the shipment. It is recommended that final inspection checklists be developed and utilized.

Education and training programs should be established as necessary to ensure effective performance of shipping personnel.

- Communications

Product safety should periodically be an agenda item for operations and staff meetings at all organization levels.

A program for timely investigation and dissemination of information regarding product incidents, safety suggestions, complaints, accidents, and claims should be developed and communicated throughout all departments and field activities.

- Complaints and Claim Handling

The definition of a complaint or claim, for the purposes of this program, is any verbal or written report of personal injury, property damage, or other claimed loss allegedly resulting from a direct or related failure of any company-provided material, product, work, or service. Also include for control purposes all apparent or alleged malfunctions or failures regardless of the presence of an actual claim for loss.

Conversely, complaints of claims that do not relate to the functional use or safety of a product should be excluded.

A written procedure for handling product or service complaints and claims should be developed. Included should be effective controls to ensure that:

- All complaints and claims are immediately referred to an individual expressly designated to receive claims.
- Each incident is properly described and accurately recorded.
- All complaints and claims are immediately recorded on an incident log.
- Each complaint or claim is promptly and thoroughly investigated and processed.
- Whenever possible, the product is obtained for examination.
- Each incident is reviewed by the Product Loss Control Committee
- A determination of action necessary is made and corrective action taken
- All employees, sales representatives, dealers, and installation and service personnel are informed of the procedure for handling complaints and claims
- All information relating to complaints and claims and subsequent investigations, discussions, decisions, and corrective or follow-up activity is properly recorded and preserved

[NOTE: ADD MORE CONTROLS HERE]

- Claim Processing

All claims are to be processed in accordance with the Company's rules and regulations. Immediate notification by telephone is required on all bodily injury and serious property damage liability claims.

Internal reporting procedures should be developed to ensure that all claims are properly processed.

The names of individuals assigned reporting responsibilities should be properly communicated.

- Record Keeping

Formal guidelines should be established for record retention. Specific instructions should be communicated to employees for their guidance in dealing with the preparation, storage, and retention of records, samples, and test results that are related to product/service loss control.

The basic "rule of thumb" for record retention is at least the life of the product.

Product/service loss control records should not be destroyed without the express permission of the Products Loss Control – Claim Defense Committee. If in doubt the Committee should seek counsel's advice.

- LEGAL

Legal counsel should be utilized to alert the Products Loss Control – Claim Defense Committee and local management of existing laws and changes affecting Product Loss Control.

Counsel should review all contract and sales agreements for elements of potential liability.

All printed material such as labeling, advertising, and operating or maintenance manuals should be approved by counsel. All warranties should also be reviewed.

Counsel's approval should be secured before printed material or product information is actually disseminated.

Review assistance is also available from the Company's insurance broker.

Policy Statement

_____, an operating division of _____, recognizes its responsibility to provide customers and consumers with safe and reliable products and services.

To this end, we have established a formal Products/Services Loss Control Committee. The prime objective of this group is the establishment and maintenance of an effective control program designed to eliminate or effectively control injury or loss potential. As Chief Operating Officer, I will chair this Committee.

Every employee plays a critical part in Loss Control. All employees must be committed to fulfilling customer needs with safe and reliable products and services. Please give your total support to this effort.

The importance of providing safe and reliable products and services cannot be overemphasized. If we do not maintain quality, we let our customers down. We depend on our customers for business. Show them they can depend on us, every day, in every way.

Date: (Signature)
                                   (Chief Operating Officer)

Date: (Signature)
                                   (Vice President)

APPENDIX B

Requirements for legal counsel retained by or on behalf of XYZ Company Ltd.

Note: THIS IS A SAMPLE OUTSIDE BILLING GUIDELINE FORM. YOU ARE FREE TO ADD MORE RESTRICTIONS AND QUALIFICATIONS OR DELETE AS MANY AS YOU WANT

- **Introduction**

The following guidelines and rules are designed to guide outside counsel (hereinafter, "Counsel") retained to represent XYZ Company Ltd. ("XYZ") and/or its subsidiaries and affiliates (collectively, "XYZ") in assisting XYZ to manage its legal affairs. These guidelines intend to help Counsel produce effective and efficient results for XYZ, in a fair and cost-effective manner.

XYZ may find it necessary to amend these guidelines or add others during the course of an engagement as appropriate to manage legal matters properly. Prior notice will be given and the matter discussed with Counsel if such action is deemed necessary by XYZ. Questions regarding these rules and guidelines should be directed to XYZ.

- **General Guidelines**

Media communication policy: Counsel will not communicate with any media outlet or respond to any inquiries for information from any media outlets regarding XYZ and/or its customers, claims, or other legal matters, without prior approval from XYZ. Media inquiries should be directed to Attn: GC, XYZ Law Department.

Outside Coordinating Counsel-Product Liability Matters: XYZ has selected outside coordinating litigation counsel for certain product liability matters. XYZ expects that other Counsel assigned to matters managed by coordinating counsel will:

- Provide copies of reports and other communications to coordinating counsel.
- Respond to requests for information and document from coordinating counsel.
- Work with coordinating counsel to develop XYZ's claims and defense, including, but not limited to, the following: discovery responses prepared on behalf of XYZ, depositions of XYZ personnel, discovery and investigation of claims, selection of defense experts, and challenges to adverse experts. XYZ believes that cooperation in this regard is critical to ensuring that strategies undertaken on XYZ's behalf are consistently undertaken in the various cases in which XYZ is involved.

- **Initial Requirements for New Engagements**

Engagement Letters: Unless instructed otherwise, within seven (7) days of Counsel's receipt of an assignment from XYZ, Counsel must provide XYZ with an engagement letter. XYZ expects that Counsel will not charge XYZ for the time and expenses associated with preparing engagement letters. Engagement letters must set forth the following information:

- Confirmation of the assignment and scope of work.
- Counsel's agreement to follow and abide by the within Guidelines, as well as other applicable corporate policies and procedures.
- Counsel's personnel who are proposed for the assignment and their billing rates, consistent with the within Guidelines pertaining to "Staffing of Matters."
- Counsel's verification that it has not identified any actual or potential conflicts of interest arising from the engagement or that such conflicts have been resolved in accordance with the within rules and guidelines and applicable rules of professional conduct.

Case Plan and Budget: Within fourteen (14) days of Counsel's receipt of an assignment from XYZ, Counsel must submit to XYZ a Case Plan and Budget that sets forth the following data, which XYZ will review with Counsel on a timely basis after the engagement is made:

- Counsel's assessment of XYZ's potential liability, including a discussion of the relative liabilities of XYZ and/or its subsidiaries.
- Counsel's knowledge about adverse counsel and the local jurisdiction.
- A proposed strategy for defending or prosecuting the case.
- Identification of significant activity anticipated by Counsel, including removal to federal court, factual investigation, motions and discovery, and an estimated completion date for each significant activity.
- Identification and assessment of prospects for early resolution of the case, including settlement and dispositive motion practice.
- For litigation matters, a discovery end date and an anticipated trial date.
- A budget for the anticipated work during the engagement, with apportionment of the budget to anticipated tasks.

- **Reporting to XYZ**

In addition to the initial case reporting described above, XYZ expects that Counsel will communicate with XYZ on a regular basis, at least quarterly, to apprise XYZ of significant developments that occur during a case. Counsel shall also be responsible for updating the case plan and budget quarterly. During the case, XYZ may request monthly updates on significant events or milestones identified by XYZ.

Significant events about which Counsel should report to XYZ include depositions (summaries should be provided), and summaries of expert reports, opinions, testimony, and other important events. In particular, before filing any dispositive motions, Counsel must advise XYZ of Counsel's intent to file any such motions and provide draft motion papers for XYZ's review at least two (2) weeks prior to the anticipated filing date.

Pre-trial reports: For litigation matters, unless otherwise specified by XYZ, at least ninety (90) days prior to a scheduled trial date, Counsel must submit to XYZ a detailed pre-trial report, which includes a description of the important issues for trial, and the relative strengths and weaknesses of the positions of parties regarding those issues. Thereafter, Counsel will provide monthly written status reports up to the trial date.

Copies of documents:

- Copies of the following documents, when generated, should be sent to XYZ: pleadings; orders; research memoranda (where authorized); legal briefs and motion papers; expert reports; and medical reports.
- In addition, Counsel should send transcripts of depositions of XYZ personnel to XYZ.
- Deposition transcripts should be sent to XYZ in ".txt" or ASCII format, with copies of any exhibits in Adobe PDF or ".tif" format, via electronic mail.

- Counsel should send such documents other than deposition transcripts to XYZ electronically (in Adobe PDF or ".tif" formats, via electronic mail or otherwise) wherever possible, to minimize the costs of transmission and to accommodate XYZ's electronic record keeping systems.

Budgetary matters: Counsel must contact XYZ to advise that Counsel's fees or expenses are expected to exceed the case budget or an approved updated case budget, at least fourteen (14) days prior to the rendering of an invoice containing the fees or expenses that exceed the case budget. Counsel's communication to XYZ in this regard must include the amount of the expected overage, and a detailed explanation of the reason(s) why the case budget or an approved updated case budget would be exceeded, if the overage is approved by XYZ. XYZ will review such communications from Counsel and will determine whether or not to permit the reported overage.

Counsel will respond to all other requests from XYZ for information and documents in a timely manner.

- **Staffing of Matters**

XYZ reserves the right to review and modify Counsel's proposed staffing of matters handled on behalf of XYZ. For the sake of efficiency, Counsel should make every effort to limit the number of professionals performing work on matters for XYZ to the lowest levels consistent with Counsel's professional responsibilities.

Changes to and Continuity of Personnel: Counsel must first seek and receive Samsung's permission to modify (additions and substitutions) the case staffing outlined in the initial case report. If Samsung approves such staffing changes, then XYZ will not reimburse Counsel for time associated with educating new staff members to the facts and background of the matters, unless the staffing changes are occasioned solely by substantive developments in the matters that call for the addition of personnel.

Experience levels of attorneys assigned to XYZ matters: Counsel may not assign lawyers who have less than three (3) years of experience in the field of practice relevant to a matter, without prior approval from XYZ.

Summer Associates/Interns/Clerks: The tasks performed by such personnel will not be paid for by XYZ, absent special circumstances and prior approval by XYZ.

Paralegals: Counsel will not assign paraprofessionals, paralegals, or legal assistants to matters assigned by XYZ without prior approval from XYZ.

Administrative/clerical tasks: XYZ firmly believes that administrative/clerical tasks are part of Counsel's overhead and costs of doing business, and will not be paid for by XYZ. "Administrative/clerical tasks" include, but are not limited to, filing, date-stamping, indexing, copying or scanning documents, and/or making travel arrangements.

Intra-office conferences: XYZ will compensate Counsel only for the cost of the most senior person's participation in the conference. Please note that Counsel who spend more than ten percent (10 percent) of their billable time annually on intra-office conferences will be closely reviewed by XYZ.

Multiple counsel at particular billable events: Counsel should consult with SAE regarding anticipated needs for attendance of multiple billers at particular events. Without prior approval, XYZ will compensate Counsel only for the cost of the most senior person's participation in the event.

Depositions: Counsel should consult with XYZ before scheduling, noticing, or otherwise initiating any depositions other than those already approved in the initial litigation plan. Similarly, Counsel should consult with XYZ prior to attending any depositions initiated by other parties.

[NOTE: PLACE OTHER RESTRICTIONS HERE]

- **Billing: Rendering Billing Statements/Invoices and Billing Rates**

General: XYZ reserves the right to review all charges for services and disbursements for legal work conducted on its behalf, without limitation. XYZ reserves the right to conduct on-site audits and to review Counsel's files and/or billing statements/invoices. Counsel agrees to comply with all reasonable requests for information and documents. XYZ further reserves its right to decline to pay charges that violate these Guidelines, and which are not fully explained, approved, or documented by Counsel after inquiry by XYZ.

Timing of rendering invoices: Invoices must be submitted not more than ninety (90) days after the month in which the time was accrued. The timing of the invoices is necessary for XYZ's budgeting and matter management. Counsel are advised that any time entries or invoices that are rendered outside this period will not be paid by XYZ without approval by the General Counsel.

Billing rates:

- Counsel agrees that billing rates set at the beginning of a matter will remain in effect unless Counsel submits a written request for a change or revision, and the written request is approved by XYZ. Such written requests must be submitted to XYZ at least sixty (60) days in advance of the effective date of the proposed change or revision.

- If Counsel's firm is comprised of multiple offices whose lawyers' (and other approved personnel's) billing rates vary by office, then for XYZ's matters, Counsel agrees to charge XYZ the lowest of the firm's rates for lawyers of the same level experience as those assigned to XYZ's matters, regardless of where the lawyers assigned to XYZ's matters are stationed.

Any other requests by Counsel for increases in compensation rates must be made to XYZ in writing, and XYZ must agree to such increases before such increases may appear in Counsel's billing statements. XYZ will not agree to such increases more often than biannually.

- **Billing Entries and Descriptions**

All billing statements/invoices shall be supported with details of the work performed. The details to be included are:

- A narrative description of the work performed for each specific task by the attorney or other professional performing it. The descriptions should set forth clearly the task performed and why it was necessary. For example, the following billing description, "Conference with ABC re: status," is not sufficient.
- Name or initials of the person who performed the task.
- The time spent on the task, in tenths of an hour increments.
- A summary by each attorney or other professional who performed work for XYZ during that month, showing the total number of hours billed by that person, his/her billing rate, and total charges for that person.

Single entry timekeeping is required: Each activity performed by a timekeeper must be set forth separately from other time entries. "Block billing" entries and entries that otherwise combine multiple tasks into single entries are not acceptable to, and will not be paid by, Samsung.

Use of standardized forms and pleadings: XYZ encourages Counsel to rely upon standardized forms for the creation of documents, where appropriate. XYZ may only be charged for Counsel's time to revise and modify such documents for the particular task for XYZ, and not for time spent to create the original forms.

Travel time: XYZ will reimburse Counsel for the reasonable cost of Counsel's actual time to travel to an appropriate case-related event.

- **Invoice Format**

Please address invoices to XYZ at _____ and send a hard copy of each invoice, with all documentation of disbursements made on XYZ's behalf, to _____.

- **Expenses/Disbursements**

Each disbursement shall be billed at Counsel's actual out-of-pocket costs. No markups or administrative fees may be added.

Approval by XYZ: Counsel shall not make any single disbursement of $500 or more without procuring prior approval from Samsung.

Documentation of disbursements: Counsel must provide documentation for each disbursement made on XYZ's behalf, including receipts and invoices. Such documentation must be provided to XYZ with the hard copy of Counsel's invoice sent to XYZ.

Interstate and long-distance travel: XYZ defines "interstate and long-distance travel" as travel between and among more than one state and/or intrastate travel outside a seventy-five (75) mile radius from Counsel's office. Counsel may not travel interstate or long distance without prior approval from XYZ.

[NOTE: YOU CAN PLACE MORE RESTRICTIONS ON TRAVEL HERE]

- XYZ expects that Counsel will undertake reasonable efforts to secure the most cost-effective fares possible. XYZ encourages Counsel to book travel arrangements as early as possible to take advantage of discounts for early reservations.
- Airfares: XYZ will reimburse Counsel only for economy or coach fare for approved flights within the continental USA, Asia, Europe, and Latin America; business-class airfare may be reimbursed with preapproval for overseas travel.
- Rental cars: XYZ will reimburse the charges for rental cars of midsize class or lower only.
- Meals and hotels: Counsel should use his/her professional judgment in selecting hotel accommodations and incurring expenses.
- XYZ will not reimburse counsel for the costs of travel agents.

Local and intrastate travel: XYZ defines "local and intrastate travel" as travel within Counsel's state of domicile, and other travel within a seventy-five (75) mile radius from Counsel's office. XYZ considers local and intrastate travel to be part of Counsel's ordinary overhead, and as such, XYZ will not reimburse Counsel for expenses related to intrastate travel.

Automobile travel (for other than local or intrastate travel):

- Charges for automobile travel must be accompanied by the following information: date(s) of travel; purpose; number of miles; per-mile charge; and the amounts and nature of other expenses (tolls, parking, etc.). XYZ will reimburse Counsel according to the Internal Revenue Service's maximum mileage expense rate in effect at the time of travel or Counsel's internal rate, whichever is lower.
- XYZ will not reimburse Counsel for the costs of fines and penalties related to driving and parking violations incurred by Counsel during business-related travel for SAE.
- XYZ will not reimburse Counsel for the cost of towing and repair services incurred to service an automobile during business-related travel on behalf of XYZ.

Photocopies:

- Photocopies numbering fewer than two hundred pages per billing period (usually monthly) are part of Counsel's overhead, and the cost of such photocopies will not be paid by XYZ.
- If Counsel determines that it must copy single groups of documents numbering more than one hundred pages, then Counsel must seek prior approval from XYZ, and endeavor to secure the most cost-effective means of making such photocopies. For approved photocopy projects completed internally by Counsel's firm, XYZ will reimburse Counsel at a rate of up to ten cents per page.

Legal and technical research; computerized legal research services:

- Performance of legal and technical research: XYZ hires Counsel based upon their experience, and expects that Counsel will be highly specialized and experienced in his/ her field(s) of expertise. As such, XYZ expects that it will be rare for legal research by Counsel to be required. Before undertaking any legal research, therefore, Counsel should obtain permission from XYZ, using the approval form attached hereto. In the few cases in which it is impractical for Counsel to procure prior approval, Counsel should inform XYZ as soon as possible after research has begun.
- Computerized legal research: XYZ considers charges related to the use of computerized legal research services (e.g., Westlaw and LEXIS-NEXIS) to be part of Counsel's overhead, and such charges will not be reimbursed by XYZ.

Charges for messengers, couriers, and express or overnight delivery services: XYZ discourages the use of such services and will reimburse Counsel only for such charges that are reasonable under the circumstances and directly related to the defense or prosecution of the case.

Other nonreimbursable expenses: XYZ will not reimburse Counsel for the following expenses:

- Photocopies (except as delineated above)
- Computer, e-mail, and word processing fees
- Support staff pay
- Overtime pay and shift differentials for staffers
- Charges and rent for conference rooms
- Office supplies
- Postage
- Library use and library staff charges
- Clerks (billable time, expenses, etc.)
- Proofreader charges

- Meals and food service (except during approved business-related travel)
- Taxis/limousines to and from office (even at night, except for approved business-related travel)
- Telephone charges
- Facsimile charges
- Cellular/wireless/Blackberry service charges
- Document scanning charges (unless pre-approved by XYZ)

[NOTE: YOU CAN ADD MORE RESTRICTIONS]

Experts, consultants and other professionals: Counsel will consult with and seek approval from XYZ before retaining or otherwise incurring expenses for work performed by experts, consultants, investigators, translators, or other professional service providers.

Agreement

_____ hereby agrees to abide by and follow "Requirements for Legal Counsel Retained by or on Behalf of XYZ Co Ltd."

_____ (firm)

By: _____

Dated:

BIBLIOGRAPHY

Basri, Carole. *International Corporate Practice*. New York: Practising Law Institute, 2011.

Basri, Carole, and Irving Kagan. *Corporate Legal Departments*. 3rd ed. New York: Practising Law Institute, 2004.

Collier, Paul M. *Fundamentals of Risk Management for Accountants and Managers*. Oxford, UK: Elsevier, 2009

CPSA, 15 USC Sec 2064 (b).

Donovan, Donald F., *"Introducing Foreign Clients to U.S. Civil Litigation"*, *International Litigation Strategies and Practice*, Barton Legum, editor, Chicago: American Bar Association, 2005

Fisher, R., W. Ury, and B. Patton. *Getting to Yes, Negotiating Agreement without Giving In*. 2nd ed. New York: Penguin. 1991.

Fujitsu Ltd. v. Federal Express Corp., 247 F 3rd 423 (2nd Cir 2001).

Harrington, Scott E and Gregory R Niehaus. *Risk Management and Insurance*.2nd ed. New York: McGraw Hill, 2003

Hopkins, Bryan E. *A Comparison of Recent Changes in Arbitral Laws and Regulations of Hong Kong, Singapore and Korea.* Seoul, Korea: *KLRI Journal of Law and Legislation* 3, no. 1 (2013).

Koltran, Phillip. *Keys to Managing a FOSS Compliance Program,* The Linux Foundation, http://www.Linuxfoundation.org.

Jacobson v. Katzer, 533 F 3rd 1373 (Fed Cir 2008).

Lewicki, Roy J, Bruce Barry and David M Saunders. *Negotiation,* New York: McGraw-Hill 2012

Littleton, Robert W., and Cherry, Thomas R. *"International Crisis Management", International Corporate Practice,* Carole Basri, editor, New York: Practicing Law Institute, 2011

Losey, Ralph C. *Introduction to e-Discovery.* Chicago: American Bar Association, 2009.

Quinley, Kevin M, *Litigation Management.* Dallas, Texas: International Risk Management Institute, Inc, 1995

Restatement of Torts (Second) Sec 402, 1964.

UCC–Sec 2-316.

UCC–Sec 2-607.

UCC–Sec 2-715.

Zubulake v. UBS Warburg LLC, 217 F.R.D. 309 (SDNY 2003).

Zubulake v. UBS Warburg LLC, 229 F.R.D. 422 (SDNY 2004).

Printed in the United States
By Bookmasters